THE BOOK
OF
KINDNESS

Also by Om Swami

1. *If Truth Be Told: A Monk's Memoir*

2. *The Wellness Sense: A Practical Guide to Your Physical and Emotional Health Based on Ayurvedic and Yogic Wisdom*

3. *When All Is Not Well: Depression, Sadness and Healing – A Yogic Perspective*

4. *A Fistful of Love: Wisdom and Humour from a Monk's Bowl*

5. *Kundalini: An Untold Story*

6. *A Million Thoughts: Learn All About Meditation from the Himalayan Mystic*

7. *The Ancient Science of Mantras: Wisdom of the Sages*

8. *The Last Gambit* (Fiction)

9. *A Fistful of Wisdom: A Monk's Light Musings on Life's Serious Stuff*

10. *Mind Full to Mindful: Zen Wisdom from a Monk's Bowl*

11. *The Children of Tomorrow: A Monk's Guide to Mindful Parenting*

Plus, nuggets of wisdom and humor served regularly on his much-loved blog: www.os.me

THE BOOK OF KINDNESS

HOW TO MAKE OTHERS
HAPPY AND BE HAPPY YOURSELF

OM SWAMI

os.me

First published in India by HarperCollins
Publishers in 2019
Worldwide rights: Om Swami Meditations, Inc.
www.os.me

The views and opinions expressed in this book
are the author's own and the facts are as reported
by him, and the publishers are not in any way
liable for the same.

Om Swami asserts the moral right to be identified
as the author of this work.

ISBN: 978-9353574109

CONTENTS
THE KINDNESS INDEX

Sunday   3

The End of Exile   15

Kindness Alters Your Brain   25

UNDERSTANDING KINDNESS

Kindness Pays   35

Charity Begins at Home   45

Worthy Recipient   55

The Opposite of Kindness   61

PRACTISING KINDNESS

The First Encounter 71

Expressing Kindness 83

A Random Act of Kindness 95

To Be Kind or Fair 101

MASTERING KINDNESS

Kindness Comes First 109

The Attitude of Gratitude 119

No Judgements 127

The Best You Can 135

The Discipline of Goodness 143

Kindness Meditation 151

Before You Go 161

Notes 167

Appendix 171

About the Author 183

THE BOOK
OF
KINDNESS

One of humankind's noblest virtues seems to arise incidentally from our sympathies becoming more tender and more widely diffused, until they are extended to all sentient beings.

– Charles Darwin, *The Descent of Man*

SUNDAY

It was the Sunday after Christmas. 26 December 2004. You can say that it started out quietly, like every other morning. Even the ocean had been unusually calm the past few days. The waves you would usually hear crashing against the sand, weren't as loud. All in all, it truly did feel like a quiet Sunday. I mean, had it not been for the birthday celebrations which had gone on late into the night, this morning would have been no different. Not only was it Jesus Christ's birthday but Ajay's daughter's, too. However, to say everything was like it had always been, would be an illusion. We get so used to life being a certain way, we forget that a new day is truly a new one.

'Can you make me a cup of tea?' Ajay called out in a groggy voice to his wife Rama, who was already up and about.

'Ssh...' she came running into the room and said, 'You'll wake the kids up.'

Their daughter, Nilya, whom they called Bulbul, had turned seven the night before, and their one-year-old son, Neeraj, slept peacefully in the next room. Safe, unaware, and wrapped in a warmth that can come only when you know that your parents are your guardians, the angels who will protect you against all odds. And Air Force Sergeant Ajay Chauhan could protect; he was tall, agile and competent.

Rama went into the kitchen to make tea while Ajay picked up the newspaper to browse through the sports section. Team India was to play against Bangladesh that day. He was sure of India's victory since they had won all the matches in the series so far. Therefore, there was a natural disenchantment while going over the cricket news. Elsewhere in the newspaper, there was a report of Atal Bihari Vajpayee's eightieth birthday celebrations and one about the securing of a cremation ground for another former PM of India, P.V. Narasimha Rao, who had died just three days earlier. There was also the news about Lalu Prasad Yadav meeting the election commissioner and some criminal snatching a bag containing ₹4.75 lakh.

Ajay got up to switch the TV on while waiting for his tea. It seemed Rama was taking longer than usual to prepare it, when he heard some commotion outside. They lived on the first floor of their building, and on the ground floor, their neighbours were having an argument. A noise of this magnitude was totally unheard of in this part of the world. After all, this was the naval air base, and the discipline, quietude and order that course through cantonments, were the norm here.

He opened the window and peeked out. Rama was already downstairs and visibly anxious.

'What happened?' he asked her, and she looked up after hearing Ajay's voice.

She raised her hand, asking him to wait, hitched her saree and ran back upstairs.

'We have to leave!' she screamed, panting and puffing. 'Get the kids.'

'Calm down,' Ajay said, while he held her by her arms. 'What happened?'

'There's a flood, maybe an earthquake,' she cried. 'We must leave right now.'

'Relax!' Ajay shook her. 'There's no river, no rain. What floods! Look at the road, it's as dry as a desert.'

'You have to trust me, Ajay,' she said. 'I felt tremors while making tea. Something bad is happening. We must leave.'

'There are no tremors during a flood! Let's have our tea.'

But Rama was not listening any more and she ran to the kids' room.

'Wake up, Bulbul!' she shook her daughter and lifted her son in her arms.

'No! It's Sunday, let me sleep,' she said, rolling over.

'Ajay! Ajay!' Rama screamed. 'Help me! Take Bulbul.'

'Okay!' he said from just behind her. He scooped Bulbul up in his arms and kissed her cheeks. 'Sorry, my daughter, but we need to go out. Your mum woke up on the wrong side of the bed today.'

They went downstairs, and it was already bustling with activity; everyone seemed to be running towards the main road. Some were shouting about floods and some, about an earthquake. Army trucks were already on the move.

'Get in, get in!' a cadet shouted, extending his hand out from the truck. All four jumped inside.

But what floods? Where? Ajay thought. The roads were completely dry.

Wham! The whole truck jolted as if hit by a charging elephant. Before anyone could figure out what was happening, the truck was submerged in water.

'Get out, get out!' the army personnel shouted. The water was rising by the second.

Ajay helped Rama, who was tightly holding onto their son, get out first. Neeraj was wailing. Next, he jumped out and got hold of Bulbul.

Wham! Another big wave came and Bulbul's hand slipped out of Ajay's. He looked in Rama's direction and then in Bulbul's. Neeraj was safe in Rama's arms and she was being helped by his neighbour whereas there seemed to be no one in Bulbul's direction. Ajay tried to run towards his daughter, but his feet were no longer on the ground, the current was taking him away. He had been trained under tougher conditions, and was certain he would save his daughter. Making his way carefully through the water, he got closer to Bulbul. Wham! Yet another wave hit him like a resounding slap. It took him a few seconds to regain his senses. There was water in his ears, nose, mouth and eyes. Salty and muddy water. Very salty and very muddy and very cold.

Once again, he swam, with more resolve, in Bulbul's direction, but she was nowhere in sight. He squeezed his eyes, trying to keep the burning sensation caused by the salt in them at bay, but he had to keep them open to spot his daughter. But it was as if she had just disappeared from the face of the earth.

Ajay heard a noise, as if he was very close to the ocean; he turned around and found himself staring at a twenty-foot high wall of water fiercely charging towards him. It was as if he was standing on the ground and looking at the roof of his two-storey home. Before he could figure out what to do, the demonic wave crashed against him, lifting and taking him with it wherever it planned to go next.

'Don't worry, I've got you,' someone shouted, as Ajay tried to regain his balance. A colleague of his had grabbed him from behind as the water around them was rising fast.

A giant tsunami had hit Car Nicobar in the Andaman and Nicobar Islands, off the Indian Coast. This had been triggered by a massive earthquake that ripped apart the west of Sumatra in Indonesia, approximately thirty minutes earlier.

'Leave me,' Ajay tried to say aloud, more saline water getting into his mouth. 'I have to save Bulbul, my daughter, she is just there somewhere!' But the man continued to pull Ajay back.

7

'Let go off me!' Ajay shouted again, but the other man knew better.

The ocean water had made devastating inroads, more than 1.2 kilometres from the coast. The entire air base was flooded. The water level had risen more than twenty feet.

Soon, Ajay was taken to a dry area. Everything around had been destroyed. As if Mahakala had run through the area, like it was an apocalypse. The tidal waves of the tsunami had torn up homes, like they were made out of paper; ripped apart jetties; smashed fishing boats; reduced coconut trees to twigs.

An emergency area was set up as a temporary meeting point. Ajay put his head between his hands and wailed inconsolably, like only a parent would.

'Bulbul doesn't know how to swim,' he howled. 'She doesn't know how to swim. She doesn't even like water.'

Everyone had their own tragedies to deal with and yet, some people around tried to console the grieving father. A bit of kindness is worth more than any precious gift when you are lost and lonely. 'Where's my wife, my son?' he asked and looked around, as if he had just woken up from a bad dream. 'Bulbul, Rama, Neeraj? Where are they? Where's my wife, my son?'

He was sobbing and repeating the words when, at a distance, he saw his neighbour on a motorcycle. His wife was sitting behind him and still holding tightly to their son. *Thank God, my wife and my son are alive. I'll find my daughter. Bulbul is brave. This water will recede very quickly.* He ran towards the motorcycle like a madman.

'Rama! Rama!' Ajay screamed at the top of his lungs. 'Thank God, you are safe. Thank God, Neeraj is safe,' he said, stopping the motorcycle. And then, he snatched Neeraj out of Rama's hands to hold him tightly, to smother him, the apple of his eyes, with kisses. Ajay kissed his son as if he'd just returned from a long war and was seeing him after years. This entire episode – from reading about the Indian cricket team to the present moment – had taken less than sixty minutes. And those sixty minutes felt like sixty years.

Neeraj's body was cold from the splashes of the tsunami water. Ajay himself was soaked, as was his wife and friend, and there was no warm blanket nearby. My son must be feeling cold, he thought. And he cast a glance here and there to see if there was any dry or warm clothing nearby. But Neeraj seemed unaffected, even at peace.

'You okay, my baby, my son?' Ajay asked, stroking Neeraj's soft hair and gently stroking his cold scalp.

Of course, Neeraj didn't respond; the boy was only one year old and hadn't yet started talking.

He never would.

His body wasn't cold from the lack of heat but life.

Neeraj was dead.

It took Ajay a minute to realize that. He frantically tried to revive him by performing CPR on him. They rushed him to the doctor in the camp, who declared him dead.

Between anxiety and disbelief, hope and loss, between sorrow and despair, celebrations and mourning, Ajay and Rama lived an entire lifetime in a few hours.

Like scavengers searching for food, they scoured the island, looking for their daughter. Rama was too shocked to do much more; her son had died in her own arms. But Ajay wasn't ready to give up. He could have saved his daughter. How could he have let her hand slip out of his? He was a marine par excellence, fit and strong. He had clambered down into ocean waters from planes, he could run up an almost vertical wall, and here he was, incapable of holding on to a tender, little hand. No, it couldn't be right.

The next day, due to a mandatory evacuation order, they were airlifted from Car Nicobar and shifted to a base in Chennai. Without their son, and without their daughter. But they were not alone. Immense grief, pain and unbearable sadness huddled around them, keeping them company.

Ajay's story doesn't end here. Years later, he met me and narrated this horror in person. He had come to me with hope. Great hope. With a feeling that I might be able to help him trace his daughter. I'll tell you what happened, but more than the story, it's the message I want to share.

When you look around, what do you see? Happy faces, smiling couples, tense looks or anxious people? Maybe all of these? Since childhood, we are told to be strong, to put on a brave face, to not cry or complain. We must not come across as weak to the rest of the world because the weak get exploited, they get crushed. It's survival of the fittest, they say. In trying to be strong, however, sometimes we become so strong that we become indifferent. Indifferent and insensitive to our own pain and to the pain of others around us. And to feel that bliss again, the kind we did as small children without a care in the world (not including our parents' scolding or beatings), we try all sorts of things. From marijuana to meditation, from detachment through yoga to indulgence in youth, from blue pills to sleeping pills and everything in between.

True, or lasting happiness, however, still remains elusive. Do you ever wonder why? I have met thousands of people who have followed their religions, lived 'by the book', tried meditating and yet, sadness seems like a disgruntled ex who won't stop stalking you. Is there an answer to this? Maybe not. But I do have some learnings. Forget all that you know for a moment, put aside your religious and moral precepts, and let's not get into what is right or wrong for the time being. Let's walk away from the concepts we grew up reading in scriptures or yogic books.

Let me share with you the science of happiness. Don't get me wrong – there's always room for meditation, faith and your views about life. In fact, we'll be using all these, but, for now, I must continue with the most important element. Yes, more important than meditation or any yogic practice you might have ever come across.

In *Narada Samhita*, the sage Narada asks Krishna where the supreme soul lives, as he wonders how to find that supreme bliss. Krishna replies:

na aham vasāmi vaikuṇṭhe yoginām hṛdaye na ca
madbhaktā yatra gāyanti tatra tiṣṭhāmi nārada

O Narada, I don't live in Vaikuntha or in the minds of
yogis. I live wherever my glories are sung lovingly.

But what does it mean to sing his glories? Is it singing
gospel, Sufi qawwali, doing kirtan or reading scriptures
out loud? Are religious people happier than non-
believers? No, not necessarily. So, what is the mystical
path to happiness, if any?

The good news is, it is possible to experience a near-
constant flow of bliss in your life. Your situation may still
be painful, people may still hurt you, success may
still elude you, or life may still be difficult, but you will
remain steadfast in your highest state of consciousness.
And this can be achieved for the most part of your day,
nearly twenty-three out of the twenty-four hours.

As I said, please put away all that you have learnt so
far. In this book, I am not asking you to meditate, I am
not telling you how mantras can transform your life, or
how you can experience *samadhi*. People who live through
such things are only marginally better off than those who
don't. Instead, I'd like to share with you something even
more powerful and practical. It works.

Let me take you back to Ajay's story. His could have
been anyone's story; yours, mine or someone else's. If my
message finds its way into your heart, the rest will come to
you naturally, because accomplishing any feat becomes a

whole lot easier once you have your heart set on it. And it is your heart we need to look into. Your mind is fine. It can focus, think, process, analyse, internalize. But it is your heart that interests me. That's where everything builds up. The brain only processes what the heart is feeling. And our heart can feel a million things in just one day. We just need to connect with it, so it feels the one thing that matters most.

I've learnt that people will forget what you said,
people will forget what you did, but people will
never forget how you made them feel.

– Maya Angelou

THE END OF EXILE

It had been more than twelve years since 26 December 2004 and more than twelve years since Ajay had slept peacefully at night. Every time he got time off from work, he would run to various relief camps, NGOs, government departments and police stations to trace his daughter. Someone said they'd spotted his daughter with a group of beggars in Tamil Nadu and he rushed to that spot with his brother-in-law, making enquiries and rummaging through every piece of information he got to possibly unite with his daughter again. His Bulbul. Someone else called him and said she was seen with a tribe of nomads in Andaman and Ajay took the next flight out to be with his daughter. But each time the news wasn't accurate and he failed to find her.

'I have come to you with great hope, Swamiji,' he said. 'Please, tell me if I'll ever find my daughter.'

As I sat there listening to him, he continued unabated. 'Otherwise, I have no faith in any religious or spiritual organizations. They are just around to mint money.'

And he went on to narrate his ordeal.

'I went back to Car Nicobar a month later,' he said. 'There were tents and many camps set up. Volunteers from many NGOs and religious organizations were there. Missionaries were roaming about tending to people and telling them that 26 December had a particular significance. That they ought to accept Jesus Christ as their saviour, and immediately more relief would be granted to them in this life and the next. Doctors from MSF, an NGO, and other organizations were helping many victims. But I was just looking for my daughter, when a man clad in white came up to me.

'I showed him her picture and asked him if he had seen her or could point me to someone who might help.

'"I can help you," he said, "but this world is temporary. If you really want help, then learn to meditate and breathe properly."

'"I will," I said, "but, can you help me find my daughter?"

'"If you join our course on meditation, it'll really help you," he replied. "I'll personally speak to my guru about you and get his blessings."

'"Please, I beg you," I told him, "you can tell me about your courses later. For now, I really need to find my daughter."

'This man, Swami,' Ajay said to me, 'kept insisting that I should join their course and meditate with them. I was numb and finally, I fell at his feet and told him to just help me find my daughter.

'He then took me to another colleague of his, who was teaching meditation to a group of children nearby. She was sitting in a chair and some twenty or thirty young children were following her instructions. He gave her my daughter's picture, while I looked at the kids, scanning, hoping I might find my Bulbul. She wasn't there. And then I looked at the man who was indicating something to this lady with a twitch of his eye. He stopped, as if suddenly realizing that I was no longer looking at the children but at him. And then came the statement that changed my life.

'"I've seen this girl," the woman said.

'I just broke down as soon as she told me that.

'"I saw her here a few days ago," she continued. "She was saying *mere mummy-papa mar gaye hain* (my parents are dead). I don't have anyone."

'I asked her if she could possibly tell me where my daughter might be now, but she said that no one else had seen her after that day.

'I didn't know what to think any more. Meanwhile, this man now said that since he had gotten me such vital information, I could maybe join his meditation course. I couldn't control myself and yelled at him. I went to every single person present there, asking them if they had seen my Bulbul and distributed her pictures.

'I lost my faith in all spiritual organizations that day, Swamiji,' Ajay said to me, 'because, while they were all working and helping, they were more interested in finding followers and converts.'

I told Ajay that a small group of insensitive people didn't perhaps represent their guru or their entire organization, but Ajay was past that stage where I could reason with him. I don't blame him though. When you've been running pillar to post for twelve years, you transcend theories and philosophies. You no longer want to just hear the truth, but you want to see, know and experience it now. But that's the thing; reason is the killer of empathy. When someone's down and lost, you can't use reason to pull them back. You can use some logical argument to console them a bit, but matters of the heart are best handled by the heart alone. And sometimes, all it takes is to listen to the other person, to hear them out. With Ajay, I chose this route. I was pressed for time, but his grief was so great that I didn't have the heart to tell him that I had to go.

When someone in the family dies, that tragedy turns the surviving members into the living-dead, but when you don't know if the person is dead or alive, or you hope that there's still a chance of meeting them, then it's absolutely unbearable. You die a little every day, and when you lose all energy or will to live, some news, a glimmer of hope from somewhere, resurrects you, only for you to die again when that hope fizzles out. Every rumour, every bit of news, every assurance brought Ajay and Rama back to life only to kill them again.

'So, please,' he begged, crying, 'please tell me if I will ever see my daughter again. Where can I find her?'

'Listen, Ajay,' I said to him, 'I rarely speak like this because I'm no one to interfere in the workings of Nature, nor am I big enough to do so. But I am going to offer you a direct answer because I know your daughter's disappearance wasn't your fault and you deserve some respite. Twelve years is a very long period.'

I offered Ajay a bottle of water and some tissues, and asked him to relax for a minute. A long and uncomfortable minute passed for him.

'I'm sorry to tell you,' I said, 'but your daughter is no more. She died that very day. On 26 December 2004.'

'But that lady and the others around her claimed they saw her!'

'They were telling lies.'

'But why would they?'

'I know you don't want to believe it, but I have no reason to not tell you the truth as I see it. What if I told you about two marks on your daughter's body? Will that convince you?'

He replied that it would make him more than a believer. And I then proceeded to do something I'd never done just to convince someone of something. I told him of two specific birthmarks on his daughter's body. How did I know? I really don't know myself! Call it intuitive guidance or anything else you wish. One of those signs, he knew and confirmed right away, but the other one he wasn't so sure about, because it was supposed to be on her back. Slightly stunned by this information, he believed me already. I asked him to call his wife and confirm the second sign as well. He stepped out, made the call, came back in and broke down. I tried to console him, but he cried the tears of a man who had just been set free after serving a sentence for a crime he hadn't committed. He had been wrongly convicted.

The next morning, when I met Ajay again, there was peace and serenity on his face. It was as if I was seeing a different person altogether.

'After twelve years and nine months, Swamiji,' he said to me, 'my *vanvasa* has ended. Last night was the first time that I slept in a long, long while. I didn't have nightmares, I didn't wake up in the middle of the night. I just slept. No one can replace Bulbul, no one can fill the void her departure has created in my life, but I am at peace that she's gone. I am guilty I couldn't save her, but I'm no longer guilty for not being able to find her. If she were alive today, she would be nearly twenty years old. How can I ever pay you for your kindness, Swamiji? You've lifted a big burden off our souls. My wife cried the whole night. I spoke to her today, she's at peace. I'll do anything for you.'

I don't deny that had it not been for a bit of help from my intuition, I might not have been able to lift that burden off an innocent man's soul. What helped him was my intuition, I agree, but what healed him was kindness. I also want to tell you a secret. My intuition had little to do with my years of mastering meditation or tapping into higher dimensions of consciousness. In this particular case, it arose purely because, from the deepest recesses of my heart, I wanted to help this person. Prayer to the Universe gushed forth like a Himalayan stream during the monsoons.

You, too, can tap into intuitive understanding called *prajna* in the ancient texts. You can establish yourself to be in a finer state of awareness called *kootastha* in yogic texts. You can access your highest level of consciousness – they call it *nirvikalpa samadhi*, a state of mind where there's complete oneness. *Nirvikalpa*: there's no other *vikalpa* or option, one without the second. The whole universe is your playground then.

And that's the purpose of this book. To share with you what I know about building a life that's conducive to happiness, about cultivating an attitude that nurtures your intuition. To make the law of attraction work, or to gain what I wrote in the preceding paragraph, you need to open your heart to attain that divine union with the extraordinary forces of nature. No doubt that meditation helps you train and tame your mind to help you remain in a state of awareness, or that chanting mantras helps you align your energies with the cosmic vibrations. But opening your heart like a lotus in full bloom to emit a fragrance, requires practising kindness in your daily life.

It is possible to learn the art and practice of kindness in a way that it is not seen as your weakness but strength. So you stand tall on its foundation and are not crushed under its weight. So that you become a master of circumstances and are not dragged along by life and its uncertainties. All of it is possible with kindness.

Let me show you exactly how.

We can change our habits. We needn't be at the mercy of thoughts like 'that's just my personality' or 'it's in my genes so there's nothing I can do about it'. Negative habits can be replaced with positive ones, selfish ones with kind ones, suspicion with trust, hostility with empathy and complaints with gratitude.

– David R. Hamilton, *Why Kindness is Good for You*

KINDNESS ALTERS YOUR BRAIN

One of the most fascinating things about kindness is not that it is a sublime emotion or that the same part in your brain lights up when you make someone happy as it would if you experienced the same joy yourself. Kindness is a skill, one you can learn, champion and benefit immensely from.

Kai Kupferschmidt wrote an insightful and well-researched article on learning kindness and its effect on the human brain, in the *Science* magazine.[1] The article opens with the following story:

> On 20 August, a young man armed with an AK-47 and 500 rounds of ammunition bursts into the

school in Decatur, Georgia, where Tuff works as a bookkeeper. It may have ended in yet another senseless mass killing if not for Tuff's compassionate response to the gun-man, recorded in its entirety because she dials 911.

As the man loads his weapon, Tuff seeks a human connection with him. She talks of her own struggles, her disabled son, her divorce, her thoughts of committing suicide. Finally, she persuades him to lay down his weapon, lie down on the ground, and surrender to the police. 'I love you,' she says near the end of the call. 'You're gonna be OK, sweetheart.' (Only after the man is arrested does she break down, crying, 'Woo, Jesus!')

Tuff's heroic conversation, posted on the Internet, was hailed by many commentators as evidence of the power of empathy and the value of compassion. If more people were like her, there would be less violence and suffering, they say.

Citing various studies done by a neuroscientist, Tania Singer, Kupferschmidt goes on to make a persuasive case, that kindness can be practised, and doing so, puts you in a warmer space in your mind. When Singer asked a noted Buddhist monk, Matthieu Ricard, to meditate on compassion by thinking about the suffering of someone or a group of people, while under the MRI scanner, she was rather surprised to see that the areas lighting up in Ricard's brain were not the ones she had seen earlier in many subjects. Due to conscious training in loving and kindness, Ricard's brain responded entirely differently.

> The brain regions she saw light up were not the ones that she had seen time and again when subjects tuned into the sufferings of another person. Instead, areas associated with romantic love or reward, such as the nucleus accumbens and ventral striatum, were activated.

In other words, such great compassion flowed from Ricard while he meditated on a group of orphan children he had met earlier, that he was not in pain but in love. At the root of such kindness is empathy.

> Empathy is the bridge that allows us to cross into the territory of someone else's feelings.

Our brain can't really distinguish between our sufferings and those of others. This is the reason we feel the emotions we do while reading novels or watching movies. This means that if I can train my brain to be kind, then even when I face adversities, my brain is going to generate overwhelming feelings of love and bliss as opposed to pain and negativity.

Before I share with you more soul-stirring and profound stories of kindness to help you see the world from a different perspective, allow me to share an article that illustrates and supports the assumption that we can take advantage of our brain's plasticity and train it to learn happiness and kindness. Please do read through this entire section and not jump to the subsequent chapters. This article is important to understand the art and science of kindness, which will then help you train yourself to experience greater happiness. Here, verbatim, right till the end of this chapter, with permission:

Can we train ourselves to be compassionate? A new study suggests that the answer is 'yes'. Cultivating compassion and kindness through meditation affects regions of the brain that can make a person more empathetic to other people's mental states, say researchers at the University of Wisconsin–Madison.

Published March 25 in the *Public Library of Science One*, the study was the first to use functional magnetic resonance imaging (fMRI) to indicate that positive emotions such as loving, kindness and compassion can be learnt in the same way as playing a musical instrument or being proficient at a sport. The scans revealed that the brain circuits used to detect emotions and feelings were dramatically changed in those subjects who had extensive experience practicing compassion meditation.

The research suggests that individuals – from children who may engage in bullying to people prone to recurring depression – and society in general could benefit from such meditative practices, says study director Richard Davidson, professor of psychiatry and psychology at

UW–Madison and an expert on imaging the effects of meditation. Davidson and UW–Madison associate scientist, Antoine Lutz, were co-principal investigators on the project.

The study was part of the researchers' ongoing investigations with a group of Tibetan monks and lay practitioners who have practiced meditation for a minimum of 10,000 hours. In this case, Lutz and Davidson worked with sixteen monks who have cultivated compassion meditation practices. Sixteen age-matched subjects with no previous training were taught the fundamentals of compassion meditation two weeks before the brain scanning took place.

'Many contemplative traditions speak of loving-kindness as the wish for happiness for others and of compassion as the wish to relieve others' suffering. Loving-kindness and compassion are central to the Dalai Lama's philosophy and mission,' says Davidson, who has worked extensively with the Tibetan Buddhist leader. 'We wanted to see how this voluntary generation of compassion affects the brain systems involved in empathy.'

Various techniques are used in compassion meditation, and training can take years of practice. The subjects in this study were asked first to concentrate on loved ones, wishing for them to be well as well as freedom from suffering. After some training, they were then asked to generate such feelings toward all beings without concentration on someone specific.

Each of the thirty-two subjects was placed in the fMRI scanner at the UW–Madison Waisman Center for Brain Imaging, which Davidson directs, and were asked to either begin compassion meditation or refrain from it. During each state, the subjects were exposed to negative and positive human vocalizations designed to evoke empathic responses as well as neutral vocalizations: sounds of a distressed woman, a baby laughing and background noises in a restaurant.

'We used audio instead of visual challenges so that meditators could keep their eyes slightly open but not focused on any visual stimulus, as is typical of this practice,' explains Lutz.

The scans revealed significant activity in the insula – a region near the frontal portion of the brain that plays a key role in bodily representations of emotion – when these long-term meditators were generating compassion and were exposed to emotional vocalizations. The strength of insula activation was also associated with the intensity of the meditation as assessed by the participants.

'The insula is extremely important in detecting emotions in general and specifically in mapping bodily responses to emotion – such as heart rate and blood pressure – and making that information available to other parts of the brain,' says Davidson, also co-director of the Health Emotions Research Institute.

Activity also increased in the temporal parietal juncture of the brain, particularly the right hemisphere.

Studies have implicated this area as important in processing empathy, especially in perceiving the mental and emotional state of others.

'Both of these areas have been linked to emotion sharing and empathy,' Davidson says. 'The combination of these two effects, which was much more noticeable in the expert meditators as opposed to the novices, was very powerful.'

The findings support Davidson and Lutz's working assumption that through training, people can develop skills that promote happiness and compassion.

'People are not just stuck at their respective set points,' he says. 'We can take advantage of our brain's plasticity and train it to enhance these qualities.

'The capacity to cultivate compassion, which involves regulating thoughts and emotions, may also be useful for preventing depression in people who are susceptible to it,' Lutz adds.

He also states that, 'Thinking about other people's suffering and not just your own helps to put everything in perspective,' adding that learning compassion for oneself is a critical first step in compassion meditation.

The researchers are interested in teaching compassion meditation to youngsters, particularly as they approach adolescence, as a way to prevent bullying, aggression and violence.

'I think this can be one of the tools we use to teach emotional regulation to kids who are at an age where they're vulnerable to going seriously off track. Compassion meditation can be beneficial in promoting more harmonious relationships of all kinds,' Davidson adds.

'The world certainly could use a little more kindness and compassion,' he says. 'Starting at a local level, the consequences of changing in this way can be directly experienced.'

UNDERSTANDING KINDNESS

KINDNESS PAYS

My first thought was to begin this chapter with the case for kindness, how numerous scientific studies have shown its positive impact on the human brain, and how it boosts our immunity and well-being. That, in every sense of the word, it pays to be kind. But then, my inner voice told me to instead share with you a real-life story that may just reaffirm your faith in kindness or, more importantly, possibly nudge you to see kindness as a mandatory and daily spiritual practice in your life. What I state below is the complete truth without a tinge of dramatization.

~

'Get the hell out of here,' he screamed at his widowed mother, shoving her towards the door.

'Please, let me stay,' she begged, 'it's very cold and dark outside.'

But he was mad with rage and this wasn't the first time. Jeevan had lost his father when he was four years old. His unlettered mother had brought him up by working as a maid in people's homes. She was nearly sixty years old now and suffered from many ailments.

It was the month of January in 1995; foggy and chilly outside. This was on the outskirts of Faridabad, near New Delhi. Whatever little she had saved had been spent on buying an auto-rickshaw for her son. He was married and together with his wife, they had made it a ritual to beat up the old lady on a regular basis. Pushing, kicking and slapping her was not new, but asking her to leave in the middle of the night was something Jeevan's mother had never expected. For the next half an hour, she begged, pleaded, fell at her son's and daughter-in-law's feet to not throw her out, but she was literally kicked in return. Jeevan was drunk but I'm not sure if it is ever an excuse. So, Haldi Devi (name changed) was thrown out of the house and the door was shut on her face.

In her old saree and a worn-out cardigan, this sixty-year-old woman, completely illiterate and without a penny on her person, got up and walked a few steps. Her knees bruised, face swollen, her arms hurting from the repeated twisting, back aching from the kicks and blows now had to face the cold air that was biting at her bones.

As she walked towards the main road, in that eerie silence on a cold winter night, all she could see were the outlines of the street lights surrounded by the dense fog. At a distance, she could hear the occasional honking of trucks. She was happy to not live in a household where she was cussed at and beaten on a daily basis. But now, where could she go? What could she do? In which direction could she have gone?

Her body now trembled and her teeth chattered whenever the flow of fearful thoughts stopped. She hadn't eaten all day. She walked back home. Yes, it was her home after all; she had built it only five years ago. It was in her son's name because he is the one who had gotten it registered and had told her that her thumbprint wasn't necessary. She knocked on the door, several times. For fifteen minutes straight. Her hands numb and hurting, she cried and cried.

The son opened the door, slapped her, kicked her, called her the dirtiest of names, and told her that he would chop her into pieces and feed her to the dogs if she knocked one more time.

'Be gone or be dead,' he said and pushed her with all his might once again. Haldi Devi fell down, but stopped crying. Her eyes had turned colder than the wind outside, as she resolved to never come back to her son.

She remembered the twenty-five-year-old Naren and began walking towards his house. She barely knew him; at best, he was a casual acquaintance because Naren, too, had no support from his family and lived on whatever he could find. But he was street-smart and very kind at heart. Naren's mother had passed away when he was only six years old and after his father's remarriage, there wasn't much love at home to look forward to. They had come across each other accidentally a few days back, when buying vegetables from a cart. And Naren had said to her that if there was anything ever he could help her with, he would be most happy.

This was, however, merely a social courtesy he had extended towards her and it was not meant to be taken that seriously. Haldi Devi didn't even know where exactly his house was. She knew that he lived in some colony that was about a forty-minute walk from her place. It was already 12.30 a.m. and she walked steadily, but failed to find his home. She spent the night under a closed shop, curled up so hard that her body hurt.

She had been sleepless in the past; countless times she had been denied food and money. There was always a paucity of things in her life, but never before had she been homeless. Tonight was the first time. As dawn broke, the fog stayed on, and movement on the roads increased, she began enquiring about Naren's home. She didn't know whether he was single or married, if he lived with his parents or by himself. She only knew his name and what he looked like. Dark complexioned, and of an average height and lean build, he was a youth full of energy, who spoke fast.

Finally, she chanced upon a milkman who knew whom she was talking about and where he lived. It was a big house. She was surprised to see that a young, average-looking boy lived in a house as big as that. Hope sprung in her heart and shone in her eyes. She knocked on the door, a servant came from inside and she timidly asked if Naren indeed lived there.

'Oh, that boy,' the servant said with a disdain he made no effort to hide. 'Yes, he lives in one of the rooms. Who are you?'

'Just tell him that the lady he saw at the vegetable market the other day has come to see him.'

'I'm not his servant,' came the curt reply, and he went back in. While going back to the main complex, he took a little detour near the garden and banged hard on a door. 'Your relative is here. Next time, tell them not to knock on the main door like that.' Without waiting for any reply, he went about his business.

A minute later, Naren opened the door and came out to meet Haldi Devi.

'Mata ji,' he exclaimed, 'you are here?'

She narrated the ordeal and asked if Naren could help her in any way.

'Don't worry,' Naren replied. 'You can't live with me because I only live in a one-room rental here and the landlord will not allow it, but I'll find something for you. First, you come inside and eat something.'

Naren gave her his blanket, made her sit next to a heater and prepared for her a glass of milk with plenty of sugar and flavoured with cardamom. He then ran out and got two plates of chana-bhatura and asked Haldi Devi to eat to her heart's content. She finished both plates. The same day, he found a one-room independent accommodation for Haldi Devi and borrowed money to buy a single bed for her and basic things to get her kitchen going.

'Please stay here comfortably and without any fear,' he said. 'I never had a mother. God has sent you and I'll take care of you in the best way I can.' And every month, Naren made sure he gave her ₹5,000. At times, he wouldn't have that kind of money. He was living a hand-to-mouth existence himself. Due to his family circumstances, he had never had the opportunity to study in a school, and had to start earning a living when he was barely ten years old. His own father had asked a teenaged Naren to leave home forever because his stepmother didn't like him. Somehow, he had managed to get by and survive in this strange world. But he never shared his ordeals with Haldi Devi. He made sure that ₹5,000 reached her every month.

Two months later, she said to Naren that she wasn't comfortable being a burden, and could do the dishes at people's homes to earn some money.

'Would I allow my real mother to do that? No,' he said. 'So, as long as I'm here, I'll find a way to earn this much for you. Please, don't worry. God is very kind.'

'I don't know God,' she said. 'I've only seen you.'

Another month went by, and she again brought the same issue up saying she wanted to do something so as to be able to earn some money. After some brainstorming, she told Naren that she knew how to make pickle and could, maybe, start making it to sell to nearby homes and shops.

Naren supported her and bought the initial raw materials. Then she started making all kinds of pickles including those of mango, carrot and lemon.

Several times a week, Naren would visit Haldi Devi, check up on her, make sure she was okay, give her company, have a cup of tea and break bread with her. It took her about four years, but she became financially independent. She was now earning more than ₹5,000 per month. Throughout this period though, Naren never faltered and the money he sent, reached her every month. No matter what his own circumstances, and how many times he had to borrow from others and cut corners in his own life, he always made sure that Haldi Devi could buy her groceries and pay her rent on time.

'Whenever I die,' she said, 'please perform the last rites on me.' She wanted him to do *antyeshti*, the offering of fire to the body of the departed soul, a privilege reserved for the eldest child in the family.

∼

I titled this chapter 'Kindness Pays'. How does it do that?

Fast forward to 2019, and Haldi Devi has a chauffeur who drives her around in a BMW. She employs a staff of ninety people, all of whom are either widows or single mothers who walked out of abusive relationships. Her annual turnover exceeds ₹3 crore ($500,000). Since that fateful day in 1995, she has not seen her biological son and no matter how many attempts he made to meet her, she has told him that as far as she was concerned, he was dead and that Naren was her only son.

The kindness of one twenty-five-year-old boy not only changed the life of an elderly and helpless woman, but also contributed to the employment of ninety other people. Imagine the number of lives that were impacted.

Naren remains just as kind to Haldi Devi even today. One of the very few people (less than four) in the world from whom I don't mind receiving a material gift. Whether it's just a box of apples or upgrading my stay at the JW Marriott, his kindness seems to overflow like a bottomless ocean. I have met tons of people whose lives he has touched and he seems to have time for everybody.

Now in 2019, Naren co-owns and runs a company with annual revenues exceeding ₹750 crore ($100 million). He's the uncrowned king of apple imports in India.

His full name? Narender Anand. Yes, that's his real name.

It is easy to love the people far away. It is not always easy to love those close to us. It is easier to give a cup of rice to relieve hunger than to relieve the loneliness and pain of someone unloved in our own home. Bring love into your home for this is where our love for each other must start.

– Mother Teresa

CHARITY BEGINS AT HOME

I am not sure if charity always begins at home, but I am certain that kindness does. At home, we are in our pyjamas, at ease, displaying our most natural behaviour. Outside, however, we put on a mask so the world doesn't see our weaknesses or judge us for our limitations. If we accidentally bump into a stranger, a spontaneous apology tumbles out of our mouth as if we are the politest people on this planet. When the same thing happens at home, we rarely say sorry, worse still, we may even hold the other person responsible for not watching where they were going.

What I mean to say is that if you are not kind at home, any display of kindness outside is simply that: a display. It is not possible to start living *for* others unless we learn to live *with* others, because to live with others, we need to have kindness, empathy, love and patience. Without these virtues, two people or even a group can't be together. Living for others is not the same as living with others. The first one is borne out of a sense of sacrifice, even *sukshma-ahamkara*, subtle-ego, that says, 'See how superior or wonderful I am that I'm only living for others.' Whereas in the latter case, you are more grounded; it's a bond of love and care, and not just give and take, or give and give. Kindness at home is paramount to truly being kind.

I read a beautiful story once written by an anonymous author but doing the rounds on the Internet. It is as follows (paraphrased):

> We were a small family, just my parents and I, and every evening we ate dinner together. I must have been eight or nine when this incident happened. Mom had a long and rough day at work. Dad was exhausted as well, so we decided we'd just have some toast with jam and milk, and that would be that. Mom took to the task right away and served us both dinner.
>
> She placed a plate of jam and a charred toast in front of my dad. Not slightly burnt but a completely blackened toast.
>
> I was waiting to see if father noticed that flattened piece of charcoal for a toast and if he would say anything. But he just began eating what was served and asked me if I did my homework and how my day had been.

When mom came and sat at the table, she apologized to my dad for burning the toast and even offered to make a new one.

'But honey,' my father said, 'I love this crunchy toast. It has its own taste, like eating one made of coffee or something.'

Later that night, I went to say goodnight to my dad and asked him if he really liked his toast burnt. He put his arm around my shoulder and said, 'Your momma put in a very long day at work today and she was very tired. Besides, a burnt toast never hurts anyone, but you know what does? Harsh words!'

He continued, 'Life is full of imperfect things and imperfect people, son, and I'm hardly the best at anything. You must be patient, kind and respectful if you want to have a happy family. Life is too short to sleep or wake up with regrets and resentment.'

The first time I read this story, it reminded me of my own childhood. My father was not too different from the man in the story. It's not that he was always patient or calm, far from it in fact. Or that he didn't disagree with my mother. To date, they have their disagreements on so many things but there is this sense of respect in that difference of opinion. They don't start yelling at each other or putting the other person down. They have never stopped caring for each other.

I still remember that when they would come home from work, my father would be right there in the kitchen helping my mother. Washing and chopping vegetables, making salad for us, quickly churning butter while she would be busy cooking; he would check up on us and help us with our homework. Soon, by 8 p.m. at the latest, it would be time for dinner and we often ate in our TV room. We would eat together merrily, spreading a mat on the floor. We were not allowed to waste any food, so I always sat next to my mother because whatever I couldn't finish, I would just slip it onto her plate. And other times, my father would serve us hot chapatis one by one. My mother would be making them in the kitchen, and three of us siblings would be sitting around and eating.

Once we were done, it was time for someone to serve our father. We took turns quietly but never told him because if he heard us trying to avoid giving him chapatis, he would be really hurt. So, one day my brother would do it, another day I would, the third day my sister would, and that is how it would carry on.

Then came my mother's turn. My father tried all his life to convince my mother to eat first before everyone else in the family so she would have some energy in her body, but she never did. She said she liked to relax after eating her dinner and not work in the kitchen, so she enjoyed eating most when everyone was done. But here's the thing: it's not that my father served our mother. One of us did. Instead, he would be in the kitchen making hot chapatis for her.

'You must also have the joy of eating a fresh, hot chapati right off the griddle,' he would say. He learnt cooking so that he could help my mother.

We were not to expect our father or mother to clear up the table or the mat we'd often sit on after we finished eating. Instead, each one of us was supposed to take our own dishes and put them in the sink in the kitchen. The common utensils in the middle, like hot cases containing curries, lentils, etc. – we would all carry one by one into the kitchen. My brother, Rajan, had mastered the art of disappearing and after putting his dish in the sink, he just wouldn't return to take the rest, until some fifteen minutes later, by when everything would have been done. It's amazing how we grow and evolve in life. The same Rajan now takes care of his wife and children in the same manner, if not better, as he saw our father do.

My mother would then get a breather and no matter what my father had to say, she was insistent on doing the dishes so she wouldn't have to wake up to a dirty kitchen. The maid would come only at ten in the morning the next day, so she didn't want to leave the kitchen like that overnight or prepare our breakfast in a place that hadn't been tidied up.

Father would immediately go to the kitchen and wash all the dishes while mother would wipe down the stove and shelves. On some days, he would insist that my mother rested, and cleaned the entire kitchen himself.

Come morning, and mother was not allowed to make breakfast for us without eating hers first. He would make her a hot breakfast, serve us, and only then was she allowed to go in the kitchen, and cook and pack our lunch. During that time, we would bathe one by one and he would put talc on my brother and then me, dress us up, comb our hair, moisturize our face and we were ready to go to the school. But we never liked the way he combed our hair. We wanted different hairstyles, but that or long nails or sleeping without brushing our teeth was just not an option. We could get up late on Sundays or on public holidays, but we still had to make up our beds immediately after waking up.

'It's not your mother's job,' he would tell us.

'One must be self-dependent,' he would tell us. 'It only takes a few minutes to do your chores if you do them regularly.'

This is what I mean when I talk about kindness at home. It is more about sharing than giving. Buddha called it *maitri*, loving-kindness. This Sanskrit word means a carefree friendship. Not careless, not insensitive, just carefree, where two people are not worried about being judged by the other.

Throughout my life, I have seen my father care for my mother, but only once did I see him express that in words. It was as sweet as it was adorable.

Sometime in 2008, I was speaking to my mother in the kitchen, when my father walked in. He went closer to my mother and said, 'I love you.'

I was surprised, astonished, in fact. I had never heard him say anything like that. His love had always

50

been for practical things. He had done his masters in political science and public administration, and had only ever spoken about education and national matters passionately. He had never showed the remotest interest in poetry, art or romance. To see him express himself like that, was something completely unexpected. I looked out of the window to see whether the sun had risen in the west that day. Mother just smiled, blushed and became shy. She didn't answer or say anything and a few moments later, he said to her, 'It's not like that. You are supposed to say, "I love you too." Otherwise, it's not complete.'

Mother just wouldn't say it, but we both began to coerce and nudge her to reciprocate. She managed to say 'I love you too' and immediately began giggling. Her ears and cheeks were a tomato red by then.

We stepped out of the kitchen and sat in our living room with cups of tea, when my father began speaking.

'Yesterday, I attended a seminar by this American speaker,' father said to us.

'Really?' I asked him.

'Yes,' he responded. 'There was free entry, so I thought there wasn't any harm in attending.'

'They told us,' he continued, 'that we must express our love. That when we get up in the morning, we should tell our partners how much we love them and so on. Go say to your wives you love them and have them say it back to you. So I thought it was a good thing and I should start it.'

'We don't do that in our culture,' mother interjected.

'What's this about our culture and theirs?' father contended. 'It's just one culture – a global one. We must adopt what's good in other cultures.'

'You, Parveen,' he continued speaking to my mother, 'shouldn't be saying that. Your sons and grandchildren live abroad. Those countries have provided them with a livelihood and a great environment. We must not be narrow-minded.'

Mother still insisted on how our culture was more suited to us and therefore, that made it the best.

Father disagreed and reminded her of a time when he took her to church every Sunday and she refused to shake hands with the priest. This was before my siblings or I was born.

'How will we know if we refuse to even experience things?' he asked me, but was really addressing my mother.

'Whatever anyone may say,' mother said, 'I'm not shaking hands with another man. In our culture, we don't do that.'

'See! That's what I mean!' Father said to me, a bit frustrated. 'That's why as a nation we are lagging behind, stuck in our old ideals. We should be forward-thinking. What's the harm in shaking hands with another man, and that, too, one who is holy?'

So that's how his first expression of love was received. Not very kindly, perhaps.

This didn't deter him though, because starting the next day, for many mornings, he would say, 'I love you' to my mother and she would reply.

Kindness at home does not mean that we only say yes to the other person for fear of hurting them. On the contrary, it is to be able to disagree with them, to give them their personal space, to acknowledge them and what all they do for you. Kindness is love; it is the peaceful coexistence of contradictions and differences. It is not transactional that I'll repay every act of your kindness with one of mine.

When you act kindly at home, being kind outside is effortless. It will become your second nature. If you examine the lives of some of the greatest inventors, from Einstein to Watson, and many saints as well, from Jesus Christ and Ramakrishna, to Guru Nanak, they had at least one parent who was a very kind soul. All other virtues, all goodness, flows from real kindness and not just a display of it.

It started with a meditation camp, where Om Swami's discourses nudged me to do something for society. I wanted to but I didn't know how. And then I saw a bunch of kids playing in the park where I go for jogging.

'Do you go to school?' I asked them.

'No,' they replied unanimously.

When I asked them why, they had different reasons, all of which brought tears to my eyes. They wanted an education but had no means. The very next day, I started teaching ten students in the park. We faced a lot of challenges in the beginning as the kids were undisciplined, unruly, the weather was unfavourable and there were people who were against it.

But I always hung on to this one line I'd heard in the camp: 'Whenever you decide to do anything significant, there will be challenges; just don't give up.'

Today I teach sixty students who turn up every single day.[2]

WORTHY RECIPIENT

Something I often get asked is: 'What if you are compassionate towards someone but they don't value it?' Or 'What if they see your generosity as your weakness, should you still show compassion in that case?' These are reasonable questions but that's exactly what compassion is not – reasonable. It is, in fact, an unreasonable emotion. You see, the mind is the seat of reasoning whereas the heart is the seat of compassion. As a behaviour, compassion may well be supported by some reason, but as an emotion or a feeling, it is neither supported nor triggered by any reason. Behaviour can be deceptive but feelings cannot be artificial. They are what they are.

Having said that, if you behave compassionately (even if you don't feel it for the other person), that is still just as beautiful, because most of us have little or no control over our emotions, but we can control our actions at least. Behaviour fuels feelings. You continue to behave a certain way and before long, you'll start feeling that way. The question that remains, however, is who is deserving of your compassion? Should you still exercise it even if the other person doesn't really care about it? Allow me to share a simple but beautiful story.

A man of dishonourable reputation once approached Jesus and invited him for a meal to his house. Everyone knew that Christ would never accept his invitation; the man was a sinner and this was no secret. Or, so they thought. Maintaining his ever-serene countenance, Christ accepted the invitation while his disciples looked askance. They wondered how their lord agreed to visit the home of such a rogue.

The news spread like wildfire and after some deliberation, the village seniors decided to take up the matter with Him.

'Lord,' they said, 'there's no reason why you should visit this man. He's shunned by everyone, he has committed numerous sins. It doesn't suit someone like you to be seen with him.'

'Tell me something,' Christ said. 'Whom does a doctor visit? A sick person or a healthy one? A doctor must treat the sick. I'm here to spread the love of God and I don't know of anyone who is not worthy of it.'

When someone approaches you for something, before you reject their plea, just pause. Maybe you are bigger than their mistakes, maybe you can forgive, and maybe you can exercise compassion. This is a choice and depending on your own temperament, you are free to make a different one. When it comes to compassion though, everyone is a deserving recipient, for compassion is, once again, unreasonable. But compassion is not always unconditional. At least, not for the average person out there. And this brings me to an important point: show your compassion to the one who wants it.

Please let this sink in. Take a minute to think about it.

We don't have to judge the other person, we don't have to discriminate, but we should take it as a given that everyone deserves our compassion. However, this does not mean that you have to offer it to the one who rejects it or the one who doesn't value it. Such compassion often hurts both – the one offering it, as well as the one receiving it, because the one exercising compassion feels unappreciated and let down, and the recipient sees it as a weakness.

Even in our story, Christ did not visit that man uninvited. But once the one inviting requested His presence, Christ did not judge him based on his merit (or lack of it). Like a true sage, he agreed. Because exercising compassion is neither based on merit, nor based on the need of the other person, but based entirely on their readiness. When they approach you, they are more likely to be ready than when you offer it unasked. The emotion of compassion flourishes, benefits and survives only when the recipient is ready. And readiness is not the same as worthiness.

Imagine a patient who believes he is not sick. You can't really treat such a person because they won't take the medicine. The moment they accept they are unwell and need medical attention, they are ready to be treated. Similarly, if the other person does not want your compassion, no matter how much of it you offer him, it won't really work because they are not ready for it. No matter who you are, you have a lot to offer. Your love, time, care and wisdom need to be offered to the one who wants them.

Let me reiterate my belief: anything unsolicited, be it advice, love, help or anything else, is rarely valued. Be compassionate, but give priority to those who are ready to receive it, and who have at least asked for it. This way you are no longer judging anyone's worthiness, and yet you are being compassionate at the same time.

When you are truly compassionate, you no longer expect anything in return. Not even a thank you. Practise this in your daily life as a behaviour and eventually, it'll become your second nature. You'll feel it in your bones. Then you will know what I mean when I say that compassion is always unreasonable. Just like it is always non-judgemental, it is divine. And divinity transcends both the action and intention of the other person.

Like love, compassion is unreasonable, but unlike love, it isn't blind. Both are fulfilling though; they help you discover more about yourself, about others. Come to think of it, they are nearly synonyms. Practise one and the other shows up on its own.

In 1995, I was travelling from Hyderabad to Chennai by the second class in a train. I had just arrived from the US and had attended an interview for a position of a scientist at a prestigious defence research lab.

My co-passenger was a security guard employed in the same lab.

Back then, I ate only home-cooked food, so I avoided all vendors selling snacks and food items. When this fellow passenger saw that I had not eaten anything since afternoon, he offered me a banana, which I gratefully accepted. As I was preparing to sleep, he realized that I had skipped my dinner.

'If you have a problem with money,' he said, 'I can give you 20 rupees to buy some food. Please have something.'

How I wished that kindness be a mandatory subject in academic curricula. I was so deeply touched by his gesture and even twenty-three years later, I remember the incident vividly. Little things make a big impact.[3]

THE OPPOSITE OF KINDNESS

According to you, what is the opposite of kindness? Is it inflicting harm on someone? Not in my view.

Two years ago, I was travelling with Suvi Gargas in his car through a busy market in Patiala. I have known him for over two decades, and his devotion and love towards me baffles me to this day. In case you are wondering how we know each other, well, he married my lovely sister in 1996. A happily-ever-after story ... I digress. Presently, it was the month of June and it was icy cold. The heater was on in our car and people outside were walking about with hands in their pockets and teeth chattering. Just kidding. If you know North India (or Chennai!) then I don't have to tell you what the weather conditions were like in the month of June.

The sun was spewing fire like a giant dragon hell-bent on burning down the entire planet. We were comfortable in our car (all thanks to Mr Carrier for inventing modern air conditioning more than a century ago). People were not just sweaty, but they were singed in the scalding heat. There was not a tree, flower or even a blade of grass to be seen. All around us were only concrete shops, stressed pedestrians, haphazard traffic, unlawful carts and parked vehicles. We stopped by the roadside (perhaps adding to the list of those illegally parked vehicles) and Suvi went to the nearest pharmacy to buy lozenges for me while I sat in the car.

Casually, I looked to my left, and only about four or five feet ahead was an old lady, sitting on the pavement selling walnuts. She was guarding a small basket of her goods. I felt a wave of sadness wash over me. I wondered what her story could be. Where are her children? Can they not provide for her? Haven't we failed her as a nation? Does she manage to sell anything? Walnuts in this weather? Where did she source them from? My sadness turned into a bit of frustration, and I even felt guilty for enjoying the comforts that life has been kind enough to offer me.

Just when I was embroiled in my thoughts, a man on his scooter stopped near the lady. He turned off the engine and stretched his legs to stabilize himself, his feet touching the ground. I rolled down the window to hear their conversation.

'Are these of good quality?' he leaned forward and asked in a voice far more stern than necessary.

'Yes, sir.'

'How much?'

'₹100 for 250 grams!' she replied, taking a handful in her palm and extending it towards him so he could see the quality.

'Are you out of your mind?' the man said. 'I can buy better quality walnuts at a better price in a proper shop.'

'These are Kashmiri walnuts, sir,' the lady said, almost pleadingly.

'I would like to taste first.'

She withdrew her palm. I knew exactly what she was thinking. If every potential customer tasted her walnuts and no one bought any or only a few did, she would make a loss. She wasn't keen on giving him a walnut for just tasting it. A few seconds passed.

'You will buy, right?' she asked in a feeble voice.

'*Aur? Teri aarti karne ke liye ruka hoon*? (Why, you think I have stopped to pay you my obeisance?)

Unwillingly and a bit slowly, she cracked a walnut and gave him one half. He told her to give the other half too. The man ate the walnut, threw the shell on the road and told her that he wasn't convinced of the quality. He talked the lady into giving him another walnut, which she did. He had this authority in his voice that easily overpowered the old woman who knew that only a handful of prospective buyers would stop in a span of ten hours. She couldn't afford to lose the chance of earning her evening meal.

'Okay,' the man said, 'give me twenty rupees' worth.'

The lady was overjoyed. She immediately lifted her weighing scale, pulled out a small paper bag made from some old newspaper, and filled it with walnuts. Incredible, I thought. She would barely make a profit of ₹5 or 7, if even that, and here she was grinning from ear to ear.

'You guys are very clever,' the man said to her. 'You show one thing and sell another.'

'I'm not like that, sir. I only have this small stock right in front of you.'

'I need to taste one from the bag to ensure you haven't played any tricks!'

The lady took out a walnut from his bag, opened it and handed him both halves. Again, he ate and chucked the shells on the pavement.

'No good!' he said and started his scooter.

The lady became momentarily still, like a statue in shock. 'You can give me two rupees less,' she said, frantically putting down the bag, scooping a handful of walnuts and once again holding them out. The man was already moving. 'You can buy a smaller quantity for ten rupees,' she solicited loudly from behind. 'Five rupees!' The customer was long gone. Crestfallen, she adjusted her scale, returned the walnuts back to the small pile, folded the paper bag and slid it under the mat she was sitting on.

I got a bit upset and disturbed. I wasn't angry at that man though, for there was little to no sense in that. It wasn't like my getting cross with him would somehow make him a better human being. Nature would teach him in some other way. It always does. A minute later, Suvi came back.

'Are you carrying some cash with you?'

'Yes, Swamiji,' he responded lovingly. 'How much?'

'However much you have,' I said.

We made a quick stop at the lady selling the walnuts so she could go home for the rest of the day. To say that she was happy would perhaps be an incomplete, if not an incorrect, assessment of the situation. She was more in a state of shock. Her eyes welled up, the wrinkles on her face loosened, and she said to me that she hadn't enough stock for the money I offered her, but I told her that I didn't want her walnuts.

'*Aise hi?*' she said, wide-eyed, turning her head to one side. 'Just like that?'

'Just like that,' I said.

'*Dhanya bhag mere jo sant ke darshan hue.*' She pulled out a bag from underneath her mat and began stuffing it with walnuts. 'I'm blessed to see a saint today.'

'It's okay, Mataji,' I said. 'You can sell these walnuts tomorrow. I don't need them.'

'Please take some,' she insisted and I took one from her hand.

We rolled up the window again, she stood up with her hands folded, her back a little bent, her saree crumpled. And we drove quietly till we reached our destination. That incident made me think deeply. Who's going to repay the karma of that middle-aged man on his scooter? What price will he have to pay for that display of cunningness and insensitivity? Certainly some.

So, I ask again, what is the opposite of kindness? Is it being unkind to others? No, my friend, it goes way deeper than that.

The absence of kindness is the opposite of kindness.

Just as absence of light marks the presence of darkness, when we don't experience kindness in our hearts, we are being unkind. To be unkind is not just about acting unkindly. It is also to not be kind when we can, to simply refuse. And what is a kind act? When we act in a reasonable manner keeping the *hita* (benefit) of the other person at the fore, we are being kind. When we do so with a degree of sensitivity, caring about the sentiments of the other person, we are being kind. When we open our hearts and minds to other possibilities, we are being kind. Be firm, say no, even push back and you can still be kind. In fact, without kindness, we can't be empathic or compassionate, much less be forgiving or humble.

～

A travel agent was ecstatic looking at the bumper profits from the festive season just gone by, when he saw a little old lady and an older man longingly scanning the posters of various destinations in his shop window. Feeling generous, he called them inside and said, 'I know that perhaps on your pension you could never hope to have a holiday. But I am sending you off to a fabulous resort in Hawaii at my expense.'

They tried to turn down the offer, but the agent insisted; he said he was serious and that there was no catch. Eventually, as happy as little children who had just received new toys, the elderly couple accepted the offer and off they went. About a month later, the old lady went to that shop again.

'Tell me all about your trip!' the agent said excitedly.

'The flight was comfy and the room plush,' she said. 'I have come to thank you. But one thing puzzled me. Who was that old man you forced me to share the room with?'

Kindness does not always mean you do something without finding out what the other person actually requires. In other words, sometimes what you think is beneficial to the other person may not actually be of help to them at all. Kindness is in being sensitive and in being open towards others. For openness and sensitivity will automatically evoke the emotion of kindness in your heart.

PRACTISING KINDNESS

THE FIRST ENCOUNTER

My first brush with kindness was when I was about seven years old. Maybe it wasn't the first but this was certainly the one that left a deep, lasting impression on me and made me believe that kindness was not just an emotion but a mysterious force that completely changed the way I looked at life.

It was an incredibly hot day and even the cows and stray dogs were not to be seen anywhere in the street. They were all seeking shelter somewhere in shade. My summer vacation had started barely a week ago. Out of the fifty rupees given to me as my pocket money for the entire six-week-long school holidays, I had already spent forty-five. I don't recall exactly where I splurged my cash but my guess is thirty-five on magazines and comic books, and ten buying things from various hawkers selling tikkis, lemonade, popsicles, poppadoms, candyfloss. It resulted in me spending almost everything. Each adventure would usually cost anywhere between fifty paise to two rupees. I had been reckless with my spending because I knew I could talk my mother into giving me a bit more to get through the rest of my vacation. After all, I had already finished my entire holiday schoolwork before the vacations had even begun. Plus, she always had these small cash reserves that were big enough for me.

I remember there was a power outage, and it was not just hot, but scorching hot. We only had one water cooler but what could the damn thing do without electricity. I had already read all my magazines, comics and books. There was no cable TV back then, the radio just broadcasted the most boring classical music or old Bollywood songs that no sane child of my age could make any sense of. And again, there was no power anyway.

I opened the fridge to see if I could be delighted. But the refrigerator of a middle-class family is unable to hold many surprises. It had milk, butter, aloo-mutter my mother had made for lunch, water bottles, and a tray full of veggies. Fruits were all but finished. Oh yes, it also had a covered bowl containing the dough that would be used for making chapatis in the evening. The freezer had only trays of ice and in the face of a power cut, the melting cubes were floating around aimlessly in the trays. All in all, it had nothing of any interest. I didn't know any mantra back then to convert milk into ice-cream. (I know one now. The pandit that hands it out is called Baskin-Robbins and the mantra is money.)

I looked around in the kitchen furtively and even contemplated just eating a spoonful or two of Bournvita. My elder brother, Rajan, would usually eat half a jar in one go, if my mother ever failed to hide it before leaving for work in the morning. Bournvita was the poorer, distant cousin of a chocolate. With nothing to do or anything interesting to eat, I was bored to death and quite irritated. Now let me tell you something: it is very hard to hold on to your money, to not spend it, when you are bored. In other words, it's not possible to save when you are suffering from boredom. Plus, if you are hungry or angry on top of it, God help you.

But then, down to my last five rupees, I decided to spend it all in one go. I wanted something cold and sweet.

Coke, I made up my mind, would quench my thirst.

Just then the power came back on. Hell became heaven at the flick of a switch. The water cooler was running again, the sweat was drying. Things could not have been more perfect than to have that one bottle of coke. My first one of the season. The whole bottle to myself! I was going to enjoy it fully on my own because both my elder brother and sister, whom I used to call Didi, were visiting their friends.

I put on my shirt, slid the five-rupee-note into my top pocket and began walking towards the front door. Just then I heard a knock on the main gate. I hope it's not Rajan, I thought. If anyone, I really hoped it was Didi because she always had some extra money and I could make her feel guilty enough to lend me some, so I could get something nice to eat along with my Coke. Who wanted aloo-mutter anyway? But, if it happened to be Rajan by any chance, I was done for. He would first shower his love on you so you give him a sip. That almost always never worked. He would then increase the pressure and request, plead, appeal, cajole and threaten. That too rarely worked. Not giving up, he would then try to strike a deal. Like, he would lend me his bicycle or take me to his friend's house when they would be renting movies or give me double the share the next time he bought something. That sometimes worked. You would have to trust him at your own risk. And when all else failed, he would come into his big-brother avatar and use force, promising to take only one sip from your bottle. But the whole world knew that if he got his hands on the bottle, in one sip, he would empty half of it. And if you weren't quick enough to take the bottle back from him, you would be left with tears and maybe a few drops to lick from the bottom of the bottle.

He had already spent all his pocket money in the first two days. Don't get me wrong, he was a protective, caring and very loving big brother, and always stood by me like a rock, picking a fight with anyone who ever harassed me in any way. But, under the present circumstances, these virtues were not applicable. If it's Rajan, I thought, I would have to change my plan or warn him beforehand.

There it was again, the knock. He wouldn't knock unless he was playing a prank on me, I thought. I patted the top pocket of my shirt again, the five-rupee-note sat there safely. The pockets of my shorts were not good enough to carry anything. Why did they even bother making them like that? The moment you put anything inside and took even two steps, it would fall out.

The provision store was a mere twenty steps away. I couldn't wait to get back after buying my coke.

When I opened the main door, there was an old lady standing there. She was not even five feet tall. Fragile, petite, small, with a wrinkled face, gnarled arms and hands, in an old saree and with a steel bowl in her hand, she peered out of her small and pale eyes. Even the eyes looked old. Her head was covered with her saree. There was no sweat on her face; it had dried in that heat. I don't remember whether or not she was wearing any slippers.

She extended her bowl towards me and seeing that I was a young boy myself, there was a sense of hesitation in her asking for alms.

'I'm sorry,' I said, 'I don't have anything to give you. But if you want, I can fill your bowl with wheat-flour.'

It was a common practice to give a bowl of flour to various saints, monks, and other people who knocked at your door because they could either use it directly or sell it for a small amount. They would usually carry a bag in which they'd put the flour they received from you, mixing it with the flour received from other homes. But this old lady wasn't carrying any bag at all. I had never seen her around before.

She expressed her gratitude for the offer.

'Are you thirsty?' I asked, to which she said that she was.

'Just wait here for a couple of minutes.'

I rushed back inside my home, filled her bowl with flour and quickly squeezed a lemon in a glass, mixed it with sugar, salt and black pepper, poured cold water into it, straight from the ice tray that had nearly melted, and went outside.

'You can drink this *shikanjvi*,' I said. 'It's sweet and cold.'

She put the bowl aside, and began to take small sips of the drink from the glass. There were no beads of sweat on her forehead, but there were plenty on the chilled glass and as she sipped, I noticed she had virtually no teeth.

Without any water cooler or shade, I felt with each of her sips, a cold breeze was blowing over me, filling me up, soothing me. In the next two or three minutes, she finished the glass and then the most unexpected thing happened.

She started showering blessings on me. Non-stop. Most other alms-seeker I'd seen until this day would usually say a word or two in blessings and move on. But not her. The blessings came out of her mouth one after another. She kept saying that wonderful things should happen to me in my life, in my future. That I should succeed, shine, have a lot of money, fame, power, status and what not. She said I should have a beautiful wife and lovely children too. (Thank you, Lord, for not listening to everything she said!) I should be in good health, never run out of luck or resources and such like, she continued incessantly.

Here I was, barely seven, and I was thinking, 'Wow, she seems so happy with just a bowl of flour and a glass of lemonade.' I can't tell you the joy I experienced when I saw her this pleased. I'm sure you must know what I mean: the happiness we feel when we make the other person happy and they acknowledge it, is one of the most gratifying experiences.

I reached into my pocket and put the five-rupee-note on top of the bowl that was now filled with flour.

This gesture, as if triggering a frenzy in her, only made her utter her blessings with even more fervour. Not only did her eyes well up with tears, but they began to trickle down her face too. She continued unabated, wishing me all the good things I didn't even know one could have in their life.

I was surprised by this reaction because I had merely done what I'd always seen my mother doing. I'd simply done what the Indian culture stands for. Since time immemorial, we have received our guests warmly from all over the world. But never before had I seen anyone showering so many blessings.

I say this without the slightest exaggeration that I stood there for a good five minutes or so and she wouldn't stop. I distinctly remember feeling and saying to her, 'It's okay, it's only a tiny amount. These blessings are more than enough. Please don't stand in the sun.' But she wouldn't stop or leave. Finally, I waved at her, closed the door and walked back inside.

A little later, I went outside to check if she'd left and she had. I feel that sometimes our very first introduction to any emotion is all it takes for us to adopt it into our lives. The response we get when we display our affection, love, kindness or even any negative trait plays a vital role in determining whether we are motivated to try and cultivate those emotions in our lives or feel crushed and never show that side of ourselves (good or bad) any more. This experience for me was truly transformational. So many times thereafter, I hoped I would see her again, give her something again, hear her bless me again, but it never happened.

One year later, once again, my summer school holidays had started. I was once again richer by fifty rupees, Rajan by seventy-five and Didi by 200. Once again, I was done with all my holiday homework even before the first day of the vacation and was eagerly looking forward to some time to relax. I was home alone one day.

'I wish,' I thought, 'I could see that old woman today. I would give her the whole of the fifty rupees. If she was so moved with so little, I really wonder what she would say or do if I gave her the whole amount.'

There was a knock on the main door. I rushed to open it. I could have died out of shock.

There she was!

The same old lady.

Old saree.

Holding an old bowl.

I could not control my emotion. 'This can't be right,' I said. 'I was just thinking about you.'

She kept looking at me intently.

'Here,' I said and put the fifty-rupee-note in her bowl.

I will tell you most honestly that I don't remember everything she said, only that she said far less this time, smiled in a far more mysterious manner; there was this fire, this steely look in her eyes. As if she'd cast some spell on me, for I stood there, transfixed. I didn't have to ask her to leave. She left on her own this time. I walked back inside, not feeling as warm as I had felt the first time, but feeling empowered in a strange way. I felt I could bring some change into this world, into the lives of others. I felt I could be as wise as Chacha Choudhary and as strong as Sabu. That I could be as kind, as simple-hearted and as happy as Motu-Patlu in Lotpot. Or I could be as powerful as Krishna, who slayed the demons and fought for dharma. I felt I could be the Prahalad or the Dhruv for whom even the Supreme Soul had to manifest. I felt I could be anything as long as I remained kind.

I wasn't sure back then what God looked like, but I knew, in my child's heart, he had just visited me.

There's a famous saying in this beautiful and warm culture of ours. Yes, I know this country is fast changing, but the warmth and love you experience in India is still unlike any other place in the world. I'm not referring to just hospitality, but an underlying thread of kindness that still ties this diverse nation together. The saying goes:

Bade prem se milna sabse, is duniya mein insaan re
Na jaane kis roop mein aa jayein, Narayan ban bhagwan re

Meet everyone with love and kindness in this world, O lovely human being, because you just never know in what form God might show up.

I narrated the entire incident to my mother. She had remembered my encounter with this lady from the previous year. Not just because of the kindness but also because I had managed to weasel out ten rupees from her in the evening. So I asked if she would help me replenish my pocket money this time too, since that was all gone. She agreed to give me my fifty rupees, but split over two months, and warned me, that if I chose to give it one more time, she would not reimburse me.

That chance never came, though. I never saw that old woman ever again. I lived on the same street, in the same home, for more than eleven years, but she never showed up again.

Had that lady not returned my simple gesture with so much gratitude and kindness, had my mother not supported me, I feel I would not have tried being kind again to anyone. At least, not as liberally. And that's the thing, you see – when I talk about kindness, I'm not simply saying you should be kind to others. That comes a step later. First, you must be grateful to those who are kind to you. No matter how small an act of kindness may be on the other's part, if you don't hold back in expressing your gratitude, if you deeply appreciate what they have done or are trying to do, you will be bringing a lifelong positive change in the other person's life. This will not only help them and yourself, but also the whole world.

In my own life, I made this the benchmark. Whenever someone showed kindness to me, and I've been blessed enough to be surrounded by kind people wherever I have gone, I always tried my best to reciprocate and thank them to the best of my ability. At the core of it is this simple question: Am I poorer than even that old woman to hold back my gratitude? If she, who seemed to possess nothing, could thank me so much for such a small act, then I, who has received so much, must thank even more.

So the first step in kindness is to acknowledge more than you would care to, when someone is being kind to you.

One evening, while having a light conversation with some people, I ended up making some funny remarks about someone quite dear to me. I'd have gotten away with the misdemeanour but for the fact that I cracked the same joke again the next day. Both times in his absence. But there's only so much my conscience could take and I felt a persisting pang of unease. Imagine my surprise when the same person lovingly filled a bottle of drinking water for me just a few hours later. I had neither asked nor expected him to do so and yet, he ever so quietly performed this sweet gesture. His random act of kindness was a befitting response to my random act of cruelty. It took me a little while to figure out that we may show all the kindness in the world but the kindness that's shown to us, we can neither repay nor outdo. To be kind to others in speech and thought is not just a great service, but our duty too, I feel.[4]

EXPRESSING KINDNESS

In the ancient times, as per Vedic texts, there were three cultures that were predominant in India and its neighbouring countries. They were *devas, danavas* and *manushyas*. *Devas* belonged to the most affluent class and ruled most aspects of human lives, and in time, they ascended to higher realms. *Devas* were called gods. Even if out of goodness, they lived rather lavishly.

Danavas were the class that fought for power and wealth. However, they didn't use it for the welfare of others but for themselves. They showed no mercy. They lived mostly around the coastal region, where they acted as pirates. Over time, they came to be known as demons. Both gods and demons were born from Brahma.

Manushyas belonged to the Aryan culture and practised the Vedas. They had to strike a careful balance between the gods and the demons as they needed both in their favour to survive and thrive. *Manushya*s formed the class consisting of those we know as humans today.

They each began living in their own worlds. The gods took the higher realm, the demons took the nether world and the humans chose the middle ground – our planet earth.

Somewhere, gods, demons and humans also represent the three modes of material nature; namely, goodness (*sattva*) for gods, ignorance (*tamas*) for demons and passion (*rajas*) for humans. Passion can tilt towards ignorance or goodness, depending on how mindful we are. In other words, as humans, we have the potential to act divinely like gods or downright destructively like demons.

So, there was a time when gods, demons and humans approached Lord Vishnu for transcendental wisdom.

'We have everything,' they said, 'and yet, we are not at peace. What's the best way to live in the world?'

Lord Vishnu replied, 'You should go to Brahma. He is the one responsible for genesis, so he can guide you better because he knows the inner fabric, and this secret of the universe. What his thoughts were when he was creating this universe, only he knows. Only the artist who made the painting can tell what he was thinking when he made it.'

As per Vishnu's instructions, they went to Brahma, propitiated him and requested for an audience. He responded by telling them to come to him one by one.

'There's nothing called "absolute wisdom",' Brahma said, 'so, come to me one at a time and I'll answer your question.'

First the gods went and asked, 'How should we improve ourselves so we are happier and at peace?'

'D,' Brahma replied, and then went quiet.

The gods were a little confused because they didn't know what to make of that answer. They knew that Brahma, their grandfather, didn't like arguments or cross-questioning and that it was up to them to reject or accept the answer. They waited a little bit longer there, hoping Brahma might utter a few words more or elaborate on what he'd said, but he didn't. They did their prostration and left the place.

Next came the demons, who asked the same question and stood there reverentially, waiting to hear Brahma's answer.

'D,' Brahma replied once again and that was all.

The demons, too, stood there and waited for a little while. They nudged Brahma to say a bit more but couldn't get another word, or even a syllable, out of him.

The humans went in at the last and posed the same question.

'D,' Brahma said.

The humans, too, tried to convince Brahma to say something more but failed. Slightly confounded as well as aggrieved, they left, for the visit felt rather useless. Outside, the demons were complaining because of

Brahma's extremely short answer. The humans were unhappy, too, but the gods suggested that it was best to seek counsel from Vishnu about the meaning of Brahma's word.

'Our grandsire is too wise to say anything more than necessary,' the gods contended. 'There must be deep meaning in it.'

'Meaning my foot!' one of the demons said. 'The old man could have spoken a bit more. Did he not know how far we've travelled to just see him?'

'We agree,' the humans said, 'he could have explained his answer at least.'

As always, the gods seemed more collected while the demons fought and the humans searched for answers. Finally, at the gods' behest, they agreed to visit Vishnu again.

They eulogized Vishnu and pleaded with him to explain the significance and meaning of what Brahma had said.

'Can you believe that?' the demons said. 'That old man spoke in a monosyllable! That's all he had to say. We travelled several millions of miles to see him and that's all he said. Ridiculous!'

'But it must mean something!' the humans said.

'Pray, please don't be playful,' the gods requested Vishnu, who was also their cousin. 'Please tell us the meaning of Brahma's word. He said that the best way to live was "D". What did he mean? To each one of us, he gave the same answer, even though he insisted on meeting us separately.'

'That's because he gave a different answer to each one of you,' Vishnu said. '"D" in each case means different things.'

'Please, O Padamanabha!' they said unanimously, 'solve this mystery for us.'

'To you, demons,' Vishnu replied, 'Brahma was asking you to be more compassionate. You are always aggressive and mostly violent with the least regard for those around you. By "D" he meant, *daya*, which means compassion and mercy. You need to be more compassionate.'

'And you, gods,' Vishnu said, smiling and looking at them, 'Brahma urged you not to be so extravagant just because you can afford to be. Ostentatiousness destroys your inherent goodness. You should use your wealth and affluence to help others and not lead a debauched life. When he said "D" to you, he meant *damana*, restraint. You must exercise restraint on your opulence.'

'But what about us?' the humans asked.

'Patience, o humans,' Vishnu said, and adjusted a bit in his seat of Anantashesha.

'For you,' he continued, 'Brahma's utterance of "D" meant something entirely different. He was telling you that you are so intelligent that you can accumulate immense amounts of wealth and wisdom, but that you must pass it on for the welfare of your race. For you he meant *dana*, charity. Only by giving, will you grow.'

Gods and demons are the two sides of human beings. When you are affluent and empowered, when you are living like the gods, even if you are leading a good life, it always helps to exercise a bit of restraint for the welfare of others. When in *sattvik* sentiment (mode of goodness), exercising restraint is kindness.

In the 1960s and '70s, there was the famous hippie culture. The hippies lived how they pleased. The nature of a relationship between man and woman underwent a sea change. 'I'll rebel and do what I want to because I can', became the common mantra. There were even places where, in the name of spiritual progress, polyamorous relationships were not only encouraged but required. People smoked pot, took LSD trips, gratified themselves brazenly, but to what end? The question is, are they any happier now? In other words, excessive fulfilment of desires does not lead to lasting happiness. It is when we work towards something meaningful in life that we experience true fulfilment.

When demons are running about in our minds, when our negativity is overpowering our goodness and we feel jealous, envious of others, or we are mad at someone, at that time, we need to practice *daya*, compassion. Compassion does not mean that you don't confront the other person or that you say yes to everything. It simply means you will choose your actions and words carefully, and you will do so in a non-violent fashion.

Looking past just demons and gods, when *rajas* is predominant, which means we are in the human sentiment, we need to be charitable. Whatever we share, grows. It's the irrefutable law of the universe. Charity is an easy path for nirvana. This is easy because whatever you donate, nature secures it for you. When we eat at a restaurant, whatever we pay in our bill is an expense, but whatever we tip the server, that's our investment. That karmic investment is going to bear fruit eventually. If you give a seed to nature, to earth, it becomes a plant.

Whatever you keep for yourself, you have to make an effort to save it. And charity is not only about giving away money. That's only one small aspect of it. Sharing your knowledge is charity, putting your resources to some use so it helps others is charity.

In the Bhagavad Gita, Krishna says that a donation which is given without any ulterior motive, only for the benefit of the other person, should be given only after thinking about the place, time and the recipient of that charity. For example, if you are giving a donation to a drunkard who comes to you and says that he needs to visit the hospital, surely you will wonder if he is going to the hospital or to a bar.

The charity that is done only with the intention of helping the other person is called *sattvik*, done out of the mode of goodness. Ideally, charity should not be done blindfolded. Such charity befits the gods.

Lord Krishna says to Arjuna that a donation that is given with the expectation of something in return, or you give something out of a sense of gratitude for having received something first, that donation is governed by *rajas*, the mode of passion.

Further, Krishna says, if you are undergoing a dispute or an argument while giving a donation, this does not boost your goodness, but passion again. Any charity done out of goodness is liberating, whereas any donation given out of passion ties down the donor.

Krishna says, 'Arjuna! That donation which is not given after considering the place, time, situation and the recipient and the one who is giving the donation does not know where it is going to be used, does not know where it is going to be invested, that charity is governed by *tamas*, the mode of ignorance.'

If someone comes and requests you for some money and you give it, and they fund some terrorist activity with it, then the government will naturally come and arrest you for being the financier.

Charity done out of ignorance stresses one out, and it does not bestow peace in the heart of the giver.

In the name of religion, in our country, many people are simply running businesses. When you donate at such places, you do not get any lasting peace of mind; it exists for only a few seconds for we have done our karma, but that is not a true donation. To live a life of purity is the biggest donation. Who can give to whom, after all? Who is capable of giving to anyone? We all are blessed by nature and we are simply the medium to pass on what someone else or a group of people gave us, that maybe our parents, employers or society at large. In other words, we are all heirs.

Rahim and Tulsidas were contemporaries who lived in different cities, but both were marvellous poets. Rahim was very well-off but Tulsidas, his friend, wasn't as affluent. A commonly known fact about Rahim was that whenever he donated something to another individual, he would first lower his eyes and then make the donation.

People started saying that maybe the money he was donating was earned through bribery or some form of corruption and that was why he would lower his eyes, out of shame. Although what really happens is just the opposite. If someone is giving something from money earned illegally, they will give it with pride.

When this information about Rahim spread further, then Goswami Tulsidas wrote a letter to Rahim. 'It is being said that while giving donations you lower your eyes. Is it not pure money, or when you are donating, is it not a *sattvik* act? It is spreading everywhere that when you extend your hand to give your donation, you lower your eyes.'

To this Rahim replies:

Dene vālā koī aura hai
jo deve dina raina
loga bhrama mujhapara kare
tyoṃ tyoṃ nīce naina.

The one who is giving is that God, He gives round the clock, and people think I'm giving.

That is why as I raise my hand to give, I lower my eyes to say that please don't look upon me as the giver. What can I give? God alone is the giver.

There is no one other than Karna who can give. If you think of the definition of such a person, then it has to be only Karna in the Mahabharata. He knew that they are coming to take his protective shield, but he still gave it away. He knew that he could take everything but he did not.

So if the only basis of you giving *dana*, donation or charity is the belief that it is your money and you don't know what is happening to it, then don't think of it as a donation. Think of it as a business transaction.

I parked my car and as I got off to cross the road, I saw a scooter with two people. An elderly man was sitting at the back with his hands full of grocery bags. Suddenly, one of his slippers came off his foot. The two men stopped and waited to figure out where to put the groceries.

I felt some kindness erupt in me, and I picked up the slipper and slid it onto the elderly person's foot. He was simply astonished to see me do it. He bestowed a blessing on me, which is very special to me.

Not sure what triggered it in me, but I really enjoyed this effortless, random act of kindness where my mind did not interfere at all.[5]

A RANDOM ACT OF
KINDNESS

Nikolai Berdyaev was a Russian philosopher and existentialist. He once said, 'The question of my bread is a material question but the question of my neighbour's bread is a spiritual question.' This is kindness in a nutshell. Compassion may just be limited to a feeling, a form of empathy, a sort of acceptance, but kindness is really compassion accompanied with a gesture of giving.

An unexpected gift at an unexpected time given to an unexpected (or even unsuspecting) person with no expectations is a random act of kindness. You do it because your heart is open. Our heart has a peculiar property: it can operate in both states – open and closed. The open heart is naturally kind, compassionate and joyous. A closed heart blocks all positive emotions. It does not mean the person is negative or unsuccessful. On the contrary, a person with a closed heart can be quite headstrong, he or she may be successful in his or her career and positive about his or her material endeavours. But his or her heart remains closed to understanding and appreciating others' pain, and expressing love.

Unless you can understand another person's pain, your heart will remain closed to kindness and you will continue to be blindly focussed on your own agenda. The saddest part of a closed heart is that you only realize it when it opens. Those with a closed heart, unable to perform random or planned acts of kindness, don't even know their hearts are closed. Just like the frog in the well doesn't know a sea exists outside. It is when the door to your heart opens a bit, even just a little, that you experience a whole new world of peace and bliss. I once read somewhere, 'On the gateway of my heart I wrote, "No thoroughfare." Love came in passing by and said, "I enter everywhere."' And when love comes, it never comes alone – it brings with it tons of virtues. It is impossible to be kind without being loving.

There was once a rich man who mocked and scoffed at beggars. Anytime any beggar approached him for alms, he would chastise and cuss them; he'd tell them that they had fit bodies, were well-built, they were young and that they ought to work and not beg. This went on for a while until one day, God appeared and said, 'Listen up, you. If you don't have the heart to give, that's fine, but at least don't condemn what I gave them.'

This is another way of being kind. It's not the best, but it's second best. And that is, don't be unkind. If you can't or don't want to give for some reason, that is fine, but don't stop others, or pollute your own mind and speech by being negative about it. A random act of kindness needn't always be a material offering. Even a word of encouragement, a compliment, a helping-hand could be equally, if not more, profound.

When you regularly perform random acts of kindness, one day, something amazing happens – nature chooses you as the subject for its random act of kindness. Such kind acts are always happening in the universe, at every moment, to millions out there. Even the rains, breeze, snowfall, sunshine, flora and fauna, origination, sustenance are Cosmic acts of kindness.

A man used to give a beggar twenty dollars every month. He had been doing it for years. One time, he did not pay the beggar and told him he was sorry because he had to use the money to buy a bouquet for his wife.

'What?' the beggar asked. 'You spent my money on her?'

Just because we have something, that doesn't mean it's ours. No one is an owner in our universe, but is a medium, a custodian at the most. Whatever you share, it grows – this is the fundamental law of the universe. You share rage, that rage grows in you. You share love, it grows in you. You share contempt, then hatred grows in you. You share knowledge, and wisdom grows in you. You share your time, peace grows in you. You share what you have, and you grow as a person.

Make random acts of kindness a regular affair and nature will reciprocate.

People may say that I can't sing, but no one can say I didn't sing.[6]

– Florence Foster Jenkins

TO BE KIND OR FAIR

I'm reminded of a beautiful story called 'The Doctor's Word' written by R.K. Narayan in *Malgudi Days*. The people of Malgudi knew from years of experience that the word of Dr Raman was final. If he ever said to a patient that he wouldn't survive, without exception, that patient died within days of such a prediction. To say that people looked upon him as a great doctor would be an understatement; his prescription or prognosis was more like an oracle's word. For one thing, Dr Raman never beat around the bush and spoke only the truth to his patients.

It was only natural then, that Gopal and his family eagerly waited for Dr Raman to arrive, as Gopal lay on his bed after surviving a major heart attack. Dr Raman appeared, a bit distressed, because Gopal wasn't just any patient but his dearest friend. They had grown up together. Dr Raman checked his friend's pulse and other vitals and knew right away that Gopal was as good as dead. That he would see the sun rise the following day was near impossible.

So, when Gopal asked if he would live to see another day, the grim circumstances and grief in his family, and the faint hope in the patient's eyes, placed Dr Raman in a huge dilemma. He could break his friend and his family's hearts by telling them that Gopal would not survive, and wondered if he could tell a lie. If he told the truth, it would break them today and if he didn't, it would break them the next day. To add to it, all of Malgudi would think Dr Raman's diagnosis and assessment of the situation was wrong. His reputation would be at stake. As was his friendship. Gopal was insisting on knowing if he should sign the will because he needed to ensure he put his affairs in order before departing.

In his mind, Dr Raman had already made a choice.

He stooped over the patient and said, with deliberate emphasis, 'Don't worry about the will now. You are going to live. Your heart is absolutely sound.'

A renewed glow came over Gopal's face as he heard these words. He asked in a tone of relief, 'Do you say so? If it comes from your lips, it must be true. . .'

The doctor said, 'Quite right. You are improving every second. Sleep in peace. You must not exert yourself on any account. You must sleep very soundly. I will see you in the morning.'

The whole day passed followed by a slow night, throughout which Dr Raman was expecting to receive the news of Gopal's death, but neither did his phone ring, nor did anyone visit his clinic. I quote the final passage from the story:

> Next morning he was back at Lawley Extension at ten. From his car he made a dash for the sick bed. The patient was awake and looked very well. The assistant reported a satisfactory pulse. The doctor put his tube to his heart, listened for a while and told the sick man's wife, 'Don't look so unhappy, lady. Your husband will live to be ninety.'
>
> When they were going back to the hospital, the assistant sitting beside him in the car asked, 'Is he going to live, sir?'
>
> 'I will bet on it. He will live to be ninety. He has turned the corner. How he has survived this attack will be a puzzle to me all my life,' replied the doctor.

It is not always an easy choice: to be kind or to be fair. For instance, when a boy is singing completely out of tune or is rather cacophonous, do we tell him that he's singing terribly? Or do we say, 'Oh, don't worry, you are singing beautifully, just keep trying…'? Perhaps, the truth is somewhere in between; we must be kind, yet truthful. In other words, to be truthful in a kind way. I read somewhere that some people are so brutally honest that it almost seems that they derive more joy from being brutal than honest.

Had Dr Raman been more truthful and said to Gopal, 'Look, my friend, don't worry, the situation is dire but I think you may just pull through,' I'm sure Gopal would have seen through the doctor's lies and false assurances. If Dr Raman's lie saved a life, was it worth it? Truth be told, there's no absolute answer. Of course, it seems absolutely worth it. Is that even a question? But often the choices we have to make in our lives are not as clear-cut. Deciding whether we should be fair and speak the truth or be kind, we'll do well to remember that maybe what we see as truth is simply *our* version of the truth, if not just our perspective. Maybe Gopal didn't survive just because of the doctor's assurance but on account of his own destiny, or maybe he was just an exceptional case. We might never know, but somewhere, it's not even important.

What's a lot more important is the knowledge that irrespective of whether we choose to be kind or fair, we have a duty towards our fellow beings, to be caring, and no matter what the situation, we should never stop being gentle.

～

One day, Mulla Nasrudin slipped and nearly fell into a lake, but was caught by a friend, who was by his side, walking with him.

From then on, every time Nasrudin met his friend, whether in person or in a group, his friend would bring up the incident and remind Mulla how things might have turned out had he not been there.

A few months passed and Nasrudin could take it no more. He led his friend to the same lake and, with clothes and shoes still on, jumped right into the water. He took a couple of dips and crawled out to the shore. 'Now I'm as wet as I would be had you not saved me that day ... so stop reminding me about it!'

A kind act is a special one because it makes both the doer and the receiver feel special, but when we act kindly, in most cases, we are not doing anything special; kindness should be our first response anyway. I hear all the time from most people going through difficult circumstances about why something bad is happening to them.

'I have never done anything bad to anyone, and yet I am suffering. Why?'

First of all, I think we are cleverer than we care to admit and we conveniently forget all the instances when we acted selfishly at the expense of someone else's well-being. Secondly, and more importantly, I feel somewhat amused by their question and ask in return: 'Why? Should you be doing something bad to people? I mean, is it such a great qualification that you didn't do anything bad? Please tell me what good did you do? That's more important.'

In other words, a kind act is the least we can do to express our gratitude. Kindness is fairness. No one needs to be bludgeoned by the truth; if it's really the truth, it will unfold naturally, gently and kindly.

MASTERING KINDNESS

KINDNESS COMES FIRST

I was seventeen years old when I got a call from Henry Livingston (name changed) who was locked up in Patiala Jail. I didn't even know where this prison was.

'I'm very sorry,' he said, 'I want you to know that I am innocent.'

I stood numb at the other end of the phone. Henry was an overseas student who had come to India from Ghana. One day, eighteen months ago, when I was in Grade 11 and he was in the first year of his B.Com in the same college, I had found him sitting quietly at a street corner. I'd approached him and asked if everything was okay or if he needed any help.

He had mentioned that while all of his other friends had gotten admission in Punjabi University, he was the only one in this college. We shook hands and spent the next hour in the college canteen, eating bread pakoras and drinking tea. I even taught him a few Punjabi words!

That very day, after college, I had taken him to my house and treated him to a Fanta and some more snacks. In the evening, when my parents came back home, I'd introduced him to them and my mother cooked us a delicious meal.

Henry and I became fast friends. Every week, he would spend at least two or three afternoons at my place and once, every ten or fifteen days, I would swing by his. He introduced me to Jazz, Rap, Reggae and other forms of Western music, which were always playing in his home. He lived in a big, five-bedroom house with three other students. One of them was from Ghana too and the other two from Kenya. Except on one or two occasions, none of his other friends were ever at home.

One day, while at his place, Henry talked about having pasta, but I hadn't even heard that term before. So he painstakingly made for me a very nice dish of rice, veggies, and noodles with amazing and fresh tomato gravy. This was the first time in roughly eighteen months that I had seen him cooking anything. The next time he would make pasta for me, he said.

That next time never came.

'I was worried about you, Henry,' I said. 'I haven't seen you in the college for almost a month. I drove to your home, the door was locked and sealed from the outside, and the phone just kept ringing. Where are you? Are you okay?'

'I'm in Patiala Jail.'

'Jail!' I asked nervously.

'It's all one big mistake.'

'But what happened?'

'Mark was seeing this girl for the past couple of months,' he said. 'He recently met her at the Delhi railway station and she gave him one of her bags to take to Patiala as she was travelling with too much luggage.'

Mark Botwe was a tall man, well-built, no more than twenty-five years old, and I had met him on a couple of occasions in the past. He was pursuing an MA at Punjabi University and was one of the people who shared the house with Henry.

'I opened the door for Mark, he sat down, and soon we were surrounded by the cops,' Henry continued. 'I didn't even realize what was happening until they went through the bag and arrested both of us along with three guys and two girls who were there celebrating the birthday of one of the Kenyan boys. The luggage from that girl that Mark brought home had a bag with drugs. She was supposed to have arrived here four hours earlier than Mark, but she never showed up.'

'Oh...'

Henry assured me again that he was innocent and that he didn't know if Mark was involved either.

'I may be shifted to another jail,' he said. 'I'll call you then. If you could come and meet me just once, that'll be enough for me. That'll keep me going.'

Though I told him that I would visit him in the jail, I was extremely distressed and completely unsure of everything after Henry's call. Here was my friend in trouble and I believed him. When you are a teenager, your dreams and confusions are so great that you are willing to believe anything. I wanted to help Henry get out of jail. But what could I do?

Three days passed during which I constantly thought about Henry. I desperately wanted to know if he was all right and wanted him out. When my father came home in the evenings, he would usually ask me how my day had been and so on, but that day, he had a grave look on his face.

'Your friend, Henry,' he said to me, 'he was presented in court today. He has been charged with illegal possession of drugs.'

My father retired as Under Secretary of the State Electricity Board, and at the time, he was the superintendent of the purchasing department and was routinely required to visit the court on behalf of the organization in various civil cases where the vendors had faltered. So, he knew every lawyer and every judge in the local courts.

'I know he's innocent,' I said. 'His friend, Mark got that bag.'

He looked startled and asked me how I knew that, and I told him that Henry had called me.

'Called you!' he said. 'But this guy's been in jail for more than three weeks. He called you from there?'

Then he went quiet for a moment and asked my mother to join us, saying she should be a part of this conversation.

'Listen, son,' he said to me, 'do you realize that your association with Henry could land you in big trouble? Your whole life is ahead of you and a criminal record of any kind could destroy your career forever.'

'But I want to help him, and he doesn't have anyone here. I will go and visit him in jail,' I said. 'Shouldn't we be kind to others?'

'Are you listening to me?' he raised his voice. This was a rarity for me, because he could be upset with the whole world but only once in my life had he ever scolded me. And that had been more than ten years ago.

My eyes welled up.

He immediately lowered his voice and said softly, 'We'll help him, but we must go through a proper channel. We must respect the law. Kindness does not mean that we turn blind and lose all sense of reason.'

My father told me that he had known about Henry's arrest all along and that he had spent many a sleepless night in the past three weeks. Unbeknownst to me, he had gone through my bag, books, pockets and drawers to ensure that I wasn't into drugs. Henry's arrest had knocked the wind out of him.

'I'm sorry for not respecting your privacy,' he said to me, 'but I took your mother into confidence and only did what any responsible father must.'

'On a lighter note,' he continued, 'I'm proud of you. Your bank passbook was quite a surprise! You seem to be doing better than me.'

My father asked me to promise him that I would not speak to Henry, much less visit him, until he okayed it and that in return, he would keep me abreast of the developments in the case and do whatever he could do, ethically, to support Henry.

Henry, though, never called me again. It weighed on me that maybe I should have tried to trace him or maybe visit him in prison. Nine months later, I was taking my first flight out of the country. I was going to Australia as a student. Two months after that, Father called me to say that Henry was a free man now, acquitted of all charges. The prosecution decided not to appeal the decision. The girl was caught, she confessed to her crimes and as it turned out, it was true that not only Henry Livingston but even Mark Botwe had no clue that her luggage contained a kilogram of pure cocaine. He was just being chivalrous and helping his girlfriend.

I was relieved at the knowledge that Henry was acquitted but this news brought many questions to my mind. Even though I was going through my own struggles in Australia, I still couldn't take my mind off the fundamental question: What is kindness?

Reflecting on this only led to many more questions.

Did I not act unkindly by not visiting Henry in prison? After all, I could have made an attempt to find out why he never called me again or which jail he was in. Is kindness helping someone within your means or going beyond that? But what about yourself? Does putting your interests first mean you are being unkind?

Why should I even bother with kindness? After all, even Patanjali in the yoga sutras, as part of the first two limbs of *yama* (restraints) and *niyama* (self-discipline), talks about ten things but makes no direct mention of kindness, empathy or compassion.[7]

One day, many years later, after assiduously walking the path of meditation and material pursuits, I had a great realization, one I'm sure I'm not the first one to have experienced. It is as follows:

I can mediate till the skies crash, I can chant till the earth splits open, I can go through all the affirmations in the world and read all the self-help books or practise every form of yoga, but none of these can guarantee lasting happiness. You know why?

Unless I understand, practise and master kindness in my life, I can't experience that inner bliss. Even if I catch a glimpse of it here and there with yoga or LSD, it won't last. My personal existence must be in harmony with the cosmic existence and my selfish goals must be balanced by selfless acts. The cosmic scale has selfishness on one side and kindness on the other.

Meditation, chanting, yoga and various *kriya*s are all selfish acts geared towards my individual growth. They are based on the premise that if I'm strong and happy, I can lead a better life and help others in the process, too. But the actions above don't give us happiness. They might give you strength and fitness, yes, a promise of bliss, yes, but happiness, no. If you have practised any kind of yoga or spiritual *kriya*s then I ask you, have you found lasting happiness yet? Anyone you know who might have?

I'm not saying you shouldn't meditate or be spiritual, as I for one have devoted my life to meditation, and written books on it. All I am saying is that meditation or yoga alone is not enough.

There is only so much to gain by performing these small acts.

Kindness comes first. Always. And, a great deal of it is what we learn from observation while growing up. In other words, if we want our future generations and our existing world to be kind, we must, for starters, put kindness in our own lives first.

Doing the best we can to be there for someone is, in a nutshell, kindness.

I think we've all been in that position where we needed someone's help. We needed someone to extend that helping hand and if I can be that person to someone else, then I will definitely do it! I've learnt that everyone is the same. We're all part of the human experience and I believe that we need to look at everyone as humans and help each other the same way as we would help a close friend.[8]

THE ATTITUDE OF GRATITUDE

It is only sometimes, when we hear what others go through, do we realize what a blessed life we have.

Nine years ago, we rented a place for our business. It was a four-storey building and we had it done up according to our taste. For its upkeep, we engaged a housekeeping agency that supplied us with the right people. We were happy that we didn't have to worry about our non-core business, about training the housekeeping staff, retaining and the rest. For a bit of extra money, an external agency was accountable for all that. I sat down with one of the guys who was responsible for dusting my office – let's call him AJ – and explained to him how I wanted it cleaned. Use the Swiffer here, wet wipe there, a soft cloth here and so on.

AJ nodded throughout and carried out his task to perfection. I was impressed with this young man who seemed to be in his late teens but displayed the maturity of a senior manager. There was only one problem though. Every time he cleaned my office, the whole cabin would smell of a very strong body odour. I found it unbearable. AJ was one of the four housekeeping guys and I thought of replacing him with one of his colleagues, but I didn't want to offend him.

I wasn't sure how to broach the topic without hurting him. I asked one of my managers to gently ask AJ to take a bath every day before coming to work. AJ just nodded. A few days on, and the problem persisted. I was beginning to get irritated by his gross neglect. Once again, our operations manager had a chat with him and AJ apprised him that his agency only issued him two shirts. Instantly, we spoke to the company and offered to pay them more, provided they issued five shirts to each of their employees on our premises.

The problem was solved for a few days and then resurfaced. Our office was fully air-conditioned, so the doors were mostly closed, and every time he came to my cabin, I found it difficult to breathe for several minutes after that. We got deodorants for everyone and it only made matters worse as far as I was concerned. Firstly, the strong scent of a deodorant would trigger my allergy and my asthma would flare up. Secondly, mixed with his BO, the smell produced would be this unearthly one, from some nether world. You get the idea.

Finally, I thought I would speak to him myself. Seeing that the issue was unresolved, I (mistakenly) felt people didn't understand the gravity of the issue here. I called AJ. He looked scared.

'I'm very happy with your work, AJ,' I said to him. 'We all are.'

A big smile broke across his face. 'Thank you,' he said.

'Everyone has body odour,' I tried to explain. 'Do you wear fresh clothes and take a bath every day?'

Suddenly, his smile disappeared and he lowered his head. It took a fair bit of cajoling and prodding before he spoke. I told him repeatedly that I wasn't angry with him or firing him, and that I just wanted to understand and resolve this issue.

'Even if I want to, I can't wear a fresh shirt every day,' he said. 'I do wash my face every day when I come here.'

Temperatures can really soar in India; things can get hot and sweaty very fast. But I was appalled at his complete absence of hygiene.

'Sorry, AJ,' I said sternly, 'but you must take a bath before you leave your home every morning. It's non-negotiable.'

'But, I don't have a home, sir,' he said and began sobbing.

'Excuse me?' I asked, feeling as terrible as puzzled.

'I don't have a home,' he reiterated. 'I live in a shanty. It's made of tarpaulin and nine of us live there.'

'What?'

'There is only one water tap in our slum that has more than 500 residents living in fifty shacks. The water supply comes for two hours in the morning and evenings. Even if I wait a whole night to be in front of the queue, the big guys there will beat me up. They always get to bathe first. Even before them, the priority is given to the women filling buckets for drinking and cooking. By the time they are done, there's no water left.'

'That's awful,' I said, shocked. 'But we pay you enough so you can afford to rent a proper place, or at least a shared accommodation. You get two days off every week and ₹9,000 per month. I'm sure you can manage a better lifestyle.'

He went on to tell me that he only got one-third of that money and that he rarely ever got any day off. On his days off here, his housekeeping agency would send him to the owner's home for cleaning, gardening, etc., or at times, to some other places.

I got on the phone to the housekeeping agency and blasted them.

'Ever heard of this thing called "employment laws"?' I said to the owner. 'You guys are not running a company but a cartel.'

The owner wouldn't admit their fault and kept saying that there must be some confusion. Frustrated, I hung up. We got all the housekeeping guys together and gave them direct employment that very instant. I offered to pay for their education, and further reduce their working hours so they could go to school, college or wherever. None of them were interested in studying and I couldn't make them see the value of education. Beside gross exploitation and having to live under such inhuman conditions, their complete dislike for education was the saddest part.

On a lighter note, the BO problem was finally solved. Nevertheless, we arranged for a shower in the employees' washroom, too. AJ moved into a rental place three weeks later. It took some effort on everyone's part to find a landlord who would rent him the place because he wanted to move in with his seven family members.

I learnt a big lesson from this incident: looking at another person, we can never tell what they are going through in their lives. Many people around us live in extremely difficult, challenging or abusive environments, and often, for no fault of theirs. Putting the law of karma aside, I don't think AJ ever wished to be born into such dire circumstances, or growing up he ever imagined that this was the kind of life he had signed up for. Besides, no matter what one might have done, they don't deserve to be mistreated.

Therefore, in my humble view, our first emotion towards anyone should be compassion; let's give them the benefit of doubt. Due to our upbringing and the way our brain functions, we can't stop judging people. It comes to us naturally. We look at a man lying by the roadside and we believe he must be drunk, whereas he might have just suffered a heart attack. Based on race, appearance, clothes, speech and so on, we quickly label people. This unwholesome way of making sense of our surroundings and people around us is non-spiritual and unreasonable.

If it is spiritual progress you aspire towards, then the virtues of compassion and gratitude, of empathy and humility, have to be inculcated and practised. There is no other way. You can be firm, you can say no, you can deny a request; you can do all that and much more without foregoing compassion. If nature has blessed you with so much that you can afford to read this in a book or on a phone, tablet or a computer, somewhere then, it becomes your duty to do your bit to make this world a more beautiful and peaceful place. I'm not denying you the luxuries you enjoy in your life; you must have earned them with hard work. But that's all the more reason to do something for others. If you can accomplish so much, you can easily do just a wee bit more.

～

Once, while boarding a jam-packed train, Gandhiji's shoe came off his foot. A few seconds into his journey, he quickly took off the other shoe and chucked it onto the platform.

'What did you do that for?' a co-passenger asked him.

'At least, whoever would find them will get a pair,' Gandhi replied. 'Of what use is one shoe to anyone?'

There is no reason for us to forsake our goodness, to not count our blessings, to not help others, to not be gentle. What a blessed life we have. So let's allow others to dip into our joys and resources. The path of goodness is most rewarding for the one who seeks enlightenment.

At the beginning of this school year, my nine-year-old daughter, Payoja, had a new bus attendant. She shared with me that all the kids disliked this new bus lady because she was very strict. 'But I feel that she is a nice person,' she said.

Two days later, Payoja came home and said, 'Mumma, today when I boarded the bus, the lady was very grumpy. I hugged her and when I did that she laughed and said thank you.

I was surprised by my daughter hugging a stranger she barely knew.

One day, again Payoja hopped off the bus and showed me a pencil, and chirping as usual, she said, 'Mumma, the bus lady gifted me this pencil.'

'Oh is it her birthday?' I asked.

'No, Mumma,' said Payoja, skipping down the pathway. 'The lady said that her son lives overseas and it's the first time in the last twenty years she got a hug and a new friend.'[9]

NO JUDGEMENTS

A devout religious man completed a *sadhana* spanning forty days. At the end of his spiritual practice, he was supposed to feed someone. He tried to get the local temple priest, but he was busy elsewhere and had to turn down the offer. Just as this man was returning home, he saw an old beggar. I could invite him, he thought, after all, the same Divine dwells in all. The idea was that feeding a living soul was like feeding God and that he would earn many spiritual brownie points from such a meritorious act. The beggar, too, readily accepted the invite.

The man took him home, welcoming him with great fervour and respect. The beggar was dumbfounded at this extraordinary display of affection and reverence. It didn't just stop there; a plate full of the finest delicacies with yogurt, pickles, mangoes, sherbet, poppadoms and chutney was presented. In all of his seventy-year-long life, no one had treated him like this.

No sooner did the host put the plate in front of him than the beggar pounced on it and began devouring his meal. Indeed, it was the most delicious food he had ever tasted. The religious man, however, stood there in disbelief and confusion for a few minutes.

He then stopped the beggar from eating by holding his wrist and said, 'What are you doing?'

'Why?' the beggar asked. 'What happened?'

'What happened? What happened you ask, you thankless rascal! Aren't you supposed to say grace before you eat? Pray to the God Almighty and thank him before you eat this holy meal.'

'But sir,' the beggar said, 'I don't believe in God. I don't pray to anyone.'

The man was stunned. Distraught that his *sadhana* would be fruitless for feeding an atheist, he looked up and chanted a prayer of forgiveness. *What a sin I've committed, O Lord, by offering food to someone who negates your existence!*

'Get the hell out of my house!' he screamed, pulling away the plate of food and attempting to throw the beggar out. 'If I ever see you around here again, I'll break every bone in your body!'

'To hell with your God,' the beggar said. 'There's no damn God!'

'Get lost before I kill you!'

The beggar went away mumbling something under his breath and the man chucked the food in the trash can.

He decided to invite the temple priest the next day, or on any other he would be available, and spent the entire evening seeking forgiveness at the altar. Mad at himself and the beggar, he went to sleep at night.

In the early hours of the morning, God appeared in front of him in his dream. Amazed by this grace, he fell at his feet and clasped them tightly.

'I thought you were upset with me, O Lord,' the man said. 'I'm sorry for offering the holy meal to someone who didn't believe in you. Do teach him a lesson!'

'What have you done, my son?' God said. 'I fed that man for seventy years without judging him and you couldn't feed him once?'

~

How often have you found yourself judging someone before helping them? I don't deny that our brain largely relies on stereotypes to make sense of our surroundings with the least amount of effort, so it doesn't have to understand everything from scratch. And you have the right to discern (maybe even judge) before you perform any act of charity. But the same cannot be said about compassion, an emotion you experience in the deepest recesses of your heart, which then prompts you to act accordingly.

In an incredibly fast-paced world, where faith is fast eroding like the Arctic glaciers, it will take each one of us to do our little bit to make this world a more patient, tolerant and kind place. Just look around and you'll find that most people are not just in a rush but are increasingly restless as well. At airports, in diners, on the road, we seem to have no patience or time for anyone else. We can spend hours on our gadgets doing worthless things but won't spend even a minute on someone who needs us.

There was a time in India when people would write at the entrance of their homes: *Atithi Devo Bhava*, guest is god. Gradually, as people began placing greater importance on their own interests over community welfare, as cultures started shifting, more and more homes no longer had this saying put outside their homes. Instead, they replaced it with Namaste, signifying that you and I are one at the soul level. As a guest, you may not be God, but at least you are equally good, so you deserve my respect. As more time passed, with the dazzling materialistic progress of the Western world taking over, people began displaying a sign that said 'Welcome'. You and I are no longer the same and don't you dare see yourself as God, but still you are welcome in my home that I have built with my sweat and blood. See how successful I am.

Some more time passed and people got busier, falsely believing that happiness was an entirely individual pursuit or that they could be happy even if great disparity existed in the world around them. The welcome sign was no longer on the wall, prominent and inviting. Instead, it was then replaced by a foot mat with the same inscription. It almost said, fine, now that you are here, come inside, I'll see what I can do based on how I feel. This went on for a little while.

Now, the scene is even more different. We just put a big bold sign on our gates saying: 'Beware of Dog'.

The important thing is to be compassionate. If that is hard, just be empathic. If that's difficult too, be sensitive to others – it can be done by being mindful. If none of these seem within reach, you can be humble. If that fails too, choose to be polite. Too hard? At least be hospitable. Fine, not *atithi-devo-bhava* but hopefully not beware-of-dog either. At any rate, beware-of-the-owners is more apt, I feel.

~

A potential marital alliance had been arranged for Mulla Nasrudin. The first ever rendezvous was all set and Mulla was as eager as a bull in spring to meet his bride-to-be. All dressed up, he took two lanterns as he prepared to step out of the house.

'Where are you going with two lamps?' his father asked.

'Why, I'm off to see my prospective fiancée!'

'Son,' the father said, stroking his beard, 'when I was your age, I was so brave and so madly in love that I ran through the woods at night and met your mother in the dark.'

'No wonder, Father,' Mulla said, 'look what you got!'

If you choose to walk through your life in darkness, you will miss out on all the glory that surrounds you. And sometimes, when life forces you to pass through a dark patch, be sure to look up, for a million stars of boundless magnificence will be twinkling gently.

You won't discover the beauty of your existence till you open yourself up to new ways of thinking. To take a flight in the unchartered universe of consciousness with heightened awareness, you simply have to look at the world from a different perspective. And that's what spiritual attainment is at the end of the day: gaining a new viewpoint so you may live in the same world and yet interpret life differently. This all begins by respecting yourself and those around you, by practising loving kindness, by being humble.

No beware-of-dog. If anything, beware-of-unkind-thoughts.

The best portion of a good man's life is his little, nameless, unremembered acts of kindness and of love.

– William Wordsworth

THE BEST YOU CAN

Every now and then I like to head to Medium.com and do something akin to binge-reading. I may devote an hour or so and skim through fifteen or twenty articles. I do that once or twice a month. I particularly like this site for the quality of writing and its crisp, clutter-free user-interface. The other day, I came across a piece on kindness that brought tears to my eyes.

Written by a wonderful lady and comedian, Kristine Levine, I wrote to her seeking permission to use her article in this book. The very next day, she wrote back in a kind tone, saying yes. When I pasted the article in my manuscript and read it a second time, I was once again overwhelmed. It really felt anew all over and touched my heart in words I can't explain. The key takeaway from her article[10] is: well, why don't I share the whole thing first and then you see it for yourself? Here it is, verbatim:

I was five years old when my mom took off with me to the coast. She said she needed a do-over. We were starting fresh, with no belongings, no toys, no furniture. She said we had empty hands so that we could catch new blessings.

We also had empty pockets, and she had no job. She'd drank our whole life away, and the booze had left us washed up in a tiny beach town called Rockaway, Oregon. She was hoping the ocean would catch her tears and loosen her chains.

My mother loves the ocean. She is more herself when it is nearby. She believes that it sees and knows, that it moves and feels. It inspires her wonder and fear. She revels in the uncertainty that it could become angry at any moment and take lives at its will. To my mother, the ocean is God.

'Don't you ever take it for granted, Krissy,' she would say to me. 'When you look at that ocean, remember there's always something bigger than you. Respect her.'

Summer had just ended, and the quaint coastal town had begun to fold up. We found a small cottage – really a motel room with a kitchenette. We never said it was our home; to us, it was just 'Number Six.' My mother paid the first month's rent, enrolled me in kindergarten a block away, and bought us a sack of potatoes and some ketchup. And we began our new life.

I don't remember being excited about school. It seemed so frivolous, and I thought I should be getting a job. 'I could get a paper route,' I told my mother one night as we walked back to Number Six from the pay phone, where she'd called my dad, begging him to send the $75 child support check. He promised he'd send it as soon as possible, but I knew the potatoes were running low.

My mother looked for work, but the car we'd used to get to the town had broken down, and there were only two or three restaurants within walking distance of Number Six. She didn't want to get a job in a bar because she was trying earnestly to stop drinking.

Maybe two weeks passed and still no child support check – no money at all. I sat at the kitchen table one night, watching Walter Cronkite deliver the evening news with his objectivity and journalistic integrity. He said something like, 'Here is the news at this supper time.' I remember this because I was so surprised by it. His words were otherwise so dry, so metered, but his mention of it being dinnertime was almost friendly. I wondered if he could see us; how did he know it was time to eat?

My mother was staring out the window with her back to me. I said to her, 'Well? He's right. It is dinnertime. Right, Mom?' I thought I was being clever in catching Cronkite's sincerity.

She let out a sigh. Without turning around, she said, 'Do you see that out there? Those people have let their garden grow over. The cabbages have gone to seed now. They'd never know or care if I just snuck over and took one for you.'

The quivering in her voice scared me. She turned to me and wiped her eyes. With a look so cool I thought she might have been mad at me, she said, 'If I were a thief, I would go over there and steal those rotten cabbages for you. But I am not a thief.'

Without another word, she passed me and walked out the front door of Number Six. She left it open, and I followed her. She walked down five cottages and knocked on the door to Number One – a larger cottage, where an old man and woman lived. Even though they were our neighbours, we had no idea who they were. The old lady opened the door, and I wove around my mother so I could see inside.

'This is my daughter, Kristine,' my mother stated. 'We have no food. She's had nothing to eat but potatoes for a month, and now we don't even have any of those left. I don't care about myself, but could you please give her something to eat?'

The old woman was short and fat with dark skin and black hair twisting around her head. Her name was Anita Vanover. Her husband was a tall white man who was just called Van. I could see into their cottage; the table was set, and Anita and Van were obviously just sitting down to eat. The smells coming from inside made me drool.

I don't remember Anita saying anything to my mother or even asking her husband first if she could give us something, but I remember her packing up her table: the pot roast, the carrots, the gravy, the potatoes. She handed it all to my mother.

It turned out that the couple had friends who owned one of the restaurants where my mom had tried to get a job. Anita talked to them, and they hired her. Anita and Van became my caretakers in the evening.

They saved my mother and me.

At that moment, though, I don't think Anita and Van thought they were saving lives or forever changing the path of a child. I think they thought they were doing what they were supposed to do when a woman with a little girl comes to the door and says she needs to eat. What more needs to be said or done? They probably figured that it's just food.

When you give the best you have to someone in need, it translates into something much deeper to the receiver. It means that they are worthy.

Anita gave so effortlessly and so quickly that I doubt she ever thought about it again. But that one moment taught me a lesson about giving that I have never forgotten. There came a day thirty years later, when I passed that lesson on to my own children.

My daughter's school had a food drive, and she was excited to collect food for it. Even at ten years old, she had a strong sense of community. She wanted to be either a police officer so she could help people or an astronaut so she could protect the planet from wayward asteroids. We had to keep her from watching the news because it moved her to the point of tears. Her heart would break for the human condition.

She went to our pantry and started bagging up the canned and dry goods. All the while, she talked. 'Oh, I'll put in the green beans, I don't like those ... I'll save the Kraft macaroni and cheese. We can give them some no-name brand.' And I realized that my daughter – as generous and good as she already was – knew nothing about giving. I felt like I had taught her nothing.

She didn't know about Anita and Van. She didn't know about Number Six. She didn't know that she could see the face of a hungry child if she looked long enough at her own mother.

So I told her. I told her that my kindergarten teacher thought I was 'retarded' because I was so hungry that I didn't perform well in school and was always slower than the rest of the class. I told her that Anita could have just gone to her cupboard and made me a peanut-butter sandwich, and my mother and I would have been so grateful. But she didn't. She gave the best she had.

The biggest problem with poverty is the shame that comes with it. When you give the best you have to someone in need, it translates into something much deeper to the receiver. It means they are worthy.

If it's not good enough for you, it's not good enough for those in need either. Giving the best you have does more than feed an empty belly – it feeds the soul.

Every alternate day, a group of twenty-five people prepare and distribute khichdi (porridge) among the sick kids and patients who can't eat a proper meal but need something healthy. 'First we try to understand the need of someone who is old, ill and on medication. There are many gurdwaras that serve food, but it is mostly daal-roti. Those suffering from cancer can't eat it. So we thought of donating khichdi prepared in desi ghee with prime quality rice and lentils. It's easy to digest, good for kids, healthy for cancer patients and old people,' says Meera Goswami, a member of the group.[11]

THE DISCIPLINE OF GOODNESS

The ministers were singing glories of their king, Krishnadevaraya, the emperor of Vijaynagara. The king was bursting with joy and pride. After all, it was during his able rule that the prisons were nearly empty, the treasury and granaries full, and the taxes paid by the citizens.

'Since I'm a loving, upright and honest person at heart,' the king said, 'it is but natural that my subjects are like me.'

The courtiers agreed wholeheartedly and spoke at length of the virtues of their king. The special adviser to the king, Tenali Rama, however, kept quiet throughout.

'Why, Tenali Rama,' the king asked, noticing the disapproving look on his face, 'you don't seem too happy to hear about my qualities?'

'Who can deny your goodness, Maharaj!' Tenali Rama said, 'It's just that I think differently on this matter.'

'How?'

'Surely, your virtues matter and inspire people, but that's not the reason why they pay their taxes on time or refrain from any form of misdemeanour.'

'Then?'

'It's because we have the right system in place. Without that, things would be very different.'

'I disagree,' the king said. 'People are good because they are inherently good.'

'Sure, Maharaj. But the truth is also that people have desires and needs that repeatedly veer them off course. So much so that even the finest people sometimes struggle to put the state's interest before their own. If our governance wasn't the way it is, the very same people would behave dishonestly.'

The ministers and the king vehemently disagreed with Tenali Rama, and asked him to prove it, a challenge he took on gladly.

The very next day, an announcement was made asking people for a mandatory contribution of twenty per cent of their day's milk production for the upcoming festivities. A big vat was placed on a cart in the middle of the town and a day was set when everyone would come, get up on top of the platform and pour the milk into the vat. They were told that it was based on the honour system and that their king had full faith in the goodness and honesty of his people. Once the sun set, the cart would be pulled by the bullocks and taken to the royal kitchen.

Everyone gathered and pledged to contribute their bit. People talked amongst themselves praising their king. Some even said that they would happily give an entire day's worth of milk. The whole town was upbeat and every person informed every other.

'Where are you taking this jug?' the wife of a poor man asked him on the appointed day.

'You know where! To donate twenty per cent of today's milk production.'

'You think your one jug is going to get noticed? Who will feed our children?'

'But, I must go,' the man contended. 'All our neighbours are going.'

'Go,' she said. 'Of course, go, but let me give you the right quantity of milk.' With that, she took the jug from him, nearly emptied it and then filled it with water. 'Just put your hand in the big vat and pour it. No one will notice.'

Elsewhere in the town, a rich man was scolding his wife for filling up a big can of milk.

'If I started giving like you, soon we'll be on the streets!' He took the can from her and gave her another one that had ninety per cent water and ten per cent milk. 'It just has to look white. When the whole town is giving, one can of milk or water won't make a difference.'

Hundreds of people queued up and it was not even mid-day when the vat was already full. Another one was placed and by the time sun set, not one, not two, not three, but four vats had been filled and taken to the royal kitchen.

'Well, Tenali Rama,' the king said, pointing at the full vessels, 'see that? How charitable and kind my people are!'

'Absolutely, Maharaj. If your excellency permits, may we start boiling the milk and extract the cream, else it'll go bad in this heat?'

When they started transferring the milk into boilers, it looked much thinner than usual, as if it wasn't milk but buttermilk. Nevertheless, when the time came to extract the cream from the boiled milk, the yield was not even five per cent of the expected output.

'Maharaj,' the royal chef informed the king, 'forgive me for breaking the sad news, but the milk was anything but that. It was all just water, ninety-five per cent of it in fact.'

Krishnadevaraya was quite upset and his courtiers quiet.

'I never imagined that my people could be so dishonest. Have I been such a bad king that I couldn't inspire them to do good on their own?'

'Maharaj! Please,' Tenali Rama said, 'neither you nor our people are bad. To cut corners is human nature. Everyone thought that their little bit of milk was not important considering the entire town was contributing. And in the absence of any check, most of them merely did the formality of showing up and pouring something, even if nearly water.'

So it is with kindness; we may wonder how a little act will change the world, but it does. Every action counts. Every drop matters and every thought matters.

This write-up was inspired by the questions from a couple of users who asked in the Swaminar (using the Black Lotus app) whether small acts of kindness would actually make a difference to the doer or the world.

We tend to think that to change the world, we need something grand, something at a massive scale, one that is clearly beyond one person or a small group of people. The truth, however, is that nothing would happen if everyone thought that someone else would do it. Or what difference a small act would make. It does, it will. It always has. Whether it is a small mound or a mountain, they are both made up of tiny grains. If we took away one grain at a time, there'll be nothing left.

Goodness and kindness are nurtured by living and experiencing such virtues in our ordinary lives, in our daily actions. Gradually, they seep into our consciousness and become second nature to us. What's more, virtues are contagious. When a group of people start to live in a manner conducive to everyone's well-being and welfare, others around them adopt those ways too. No doubt, like any other transformation, it's a slow and long process, but it works. Take a look around, see how nations, cultures and religions have evolved. Some are more progressive than others.

Kindness is not charity; if anything, it's sincerity. An insincere person finds it hard to be kind or compassionate. At the end of the day, it's very simple: if you are sincere in what you do, you will be thorough in every endeavour you undertake. You realize that mastering anything, be it an emotion or a craft, requires a persistent and quality effort made up of a series of baby steps you take towards your goal.

Every kind act is a deposit in your spiritual bank account, eventually adding up.

Every small butterfly, every bee, every bird contributes to turn plain vast fields into dense forests. The tiniest amount of pollen and seeds that they carry and drop here and there, each one of those grains matters.

Why? Everything and everyone matters in this grand and incessant play of nature. You do too, as do your actions.

Let's fill our world with goodness and kindness. A lot of people need your help. Just look around and you'll know exactly what I mean.

There is a delightful scene in James Matthew Barrie's famous work, *Peter Pan*. Peter is in the children's bedroom. They're all jumping up and down with excitement. Peter has just flown across the room, and now the children want to fly too. They try to fly from the floor, then try to fly from the bed, but they can't do it.

'How did you do it?' John asks.
Peter answers, 'It's easy, John. Just think wonderful, beautiful thoughts. They will lift you off the ground and send you soaring into the air.'

KINDNESS MEDITATION

This is a short but powerful chapter. Think of this as applied kindness. In the beginning of this book, I talked about learning the art of kindness, a skill we can all master. It is. With all that I've written thus far, it gives you perspective (at least I hope it does) into how kindness can make a positive impact on your life in a big way. The meditation shared herein allows you to master kindness as a skill. You can equip your mind with kindness, so that when you step out into the world, you are a stronger and kinder person.

The kindness meditation has three stages and it should take you roughly nine minutes if you devote three minutes to each stage or fifteen minutes if you devote five. If you can find the time, then do this meditation once every day or at least four times a week. You can walk through this guided meditation in the Black Lotus app as well.

As with all meditation, sit comfortably either on a chair or on the floor. Ideally, keep your head straight, back straight, shoulders even, hands in your lap, chin turned slightly downwards, tongue touching your palate, teeth joined and lips slightly parted. If you can sit cross-legged, good, otherwise, any comfortable position will do. Start by breathing normally and gently through both nostrils. Breathe out and breathe in a few times. It's best to do this meditation with your eyes closed, but feel free to keep them open if that works better for you.

You can do this meditation with or without the support of any mantra. You can use your own affirmations or the ones shared in this chapter.

Before you do the actual kindness meditation, look inward and reach that sacred space inside your heart. You may also, if you like, use one or all of the following prayers of well-being taken from various Vedic chants:

First Vedic Chant

oṃ saha nāvavatu
saha nau bhunaktu
saha vīryaṃ karavāvahai
tejasvi nāvadhītamastu mā vidviṣāvahai
oṃ śāntiḥ śāntiḥ śāntiḥ

The meaning of the chant, alongside its simplified transliteration, is given as follows:

om saha navavatu
May Divine Grace protect both guru and disciple

saha nau bhunaktu
May He nourish us both

saha viryam karavavahai
May we work together

tejasvi navadhitamastu
May our actions be effective

ma vidvishavahai
May there be no disharmony among us

om shantih shantih shantih.
May there be peace all around

SECOND VEDIC CHANT

om bhadram karṇebhiḥ śṛṇuyāma devāḥ,
bhadram paśyemāśabhir-yajatrāḥ.
sthirair-amgais-tuṣṭuvāṁsas-tanūbhiḥ,
vyaśema devahitam yad-āyuḥ

Here's the meaning, with simplified transliteration:

om bhadram karnebhih shrinuyama devah
May we hear only good with our ears

bhadram pashyemashabhir-yajatrah
May we see only good with our eyes

sthirair-angais-tushtuvansas-tanubhih
May we lead a life of contentment and health

vyashema devahitam yad-ayuh
May we sing thy glories during the lifespan granted
to us

THIRD VEDIC CHANT

oṃ sarve bhavantu sukhinaḥ
sarve santu nirāmayāḥ
sarve bhadrāṇi paśyantu
mā kashchit duḥkha bhāgbhavet
oṃ śāntiḥ, śāntiḥ, śāntiḥ

The meaning, with its simplified transliteration, is as
follows:

om sarve bhavantu sukhinah
May all sentient beings be free of grief

sarve santu niramayah
May all be free from illness

sarve bhadrani pashyantu
May all sentient beings only see auspiciousness around.

ma kashchit duhkha bhagbhavet
May there be no suffering anywhere

om shantih, shantih, shantih
May there be peace all around

Once you have done the preliminary chant above, you are ready for the actual kindness meditation. I've particularly liked the guided loving-kindness meditation by Sharon Salzberg, so I am sharing it here with you:[12]

SENDING LOVING-KINDNESS TO YOURSELF

Keeping your eyes closed, think of a person close to you who loves you very much. It could be someone from the past or the present; someone still alive or who has passed; it could be a spiritual teacher or guide. Imagine that person standing on your right side, sending you their love. That person is sending you wishes for your safety, for your well-being and for your happiness. Feel the warm wishes and love coming towards you from that person.

Now bring to mind the same person or maybe even someone else who cherishes you deeply. Imagine that person standing on your left side, sending you wishes for your wellness, for your health and happiness. Feel the kindness and warmth coming to you from that person.

Now imagine that you are surrounded on all four sides by the people who love you and have loved you. Picture all of your friends and loved ones. They are standing around you, sending you wishes for your happiness, well-being and health. Bask in the warm wishes and love coming from all sides. You are filled, and overflowing with warmth and love.

SENDING LOVING-KINDNESS TO LOVED ONES

Now bring your awareness back to the person standing on your right side. Begin to send the love that you feel back to that person. You and this person are similar. Just like you, this person wishes to be happy. Send all your love and warm wishes to them.

Repeat the following phrases, silently:

May you live with ease, may you be happy, may you be free from pain.

May you live with ease, may you be happy, may you be free from pain.

May you live with ease, may you be happy, may you be free from pain.

Now focus your awareness on the person standing on your left side. Begin to direct the love inside you to that person. Send all your love and warmth to them. That person and you are alike. Just like you, that person wishes to have a good life.

Repeat the following phrases, silently:

Just as I wish to, may you be safe, may you be healthy, may you live with ease and happiness.

Just as I wish to, may you be safe, may you be healthy, may you live with ease and happiness.

Just as I wish to, may you be safe, may you be healthy, may you live with ease and happiness.

Now picture another person whom you love, perhaps a relative or a friend. This person, like you, wishes to have a happy life. Send warm wishes to that person.

Repeat the following phrases, silently:

May your life be filled with happiness, health, and well-being.

May your life be filled with happiness, health, and well-being.

May your life be filled with happiness, health, and well-being.

SENDING LOVING-KINDNESS TO NEUTRAL PEOPLE

Now think of an acquaintance, someone you don't know very well and towards whom you do not have any particularly strong feelings. You and this person are alike in your wish to have a good life.

Send all your wishes for well-being to that person, repeating the following phrases, silently:

Just as I wish to, may you also live with ease and happiness.

Just as I wish to, may you also live with ease and happiness.

Just as I wish to, may you also live with ease and happiness.

Now bring to mind another acquaintance towards whom you feel neutral. It could be a neighbour, or a colleague, or someone else that you see around but do not know very well. Like you, this person wishes to experience joy and well-being in his or her life.

Send all your good wishes to that person, repeating the following phrases, silently:

May you be happy, may you be healthy, may you be free from all pain.

May you be happy, may you be healthy, may you be free from all pain.

May you be happy, may you be healthy, may you be free from all pain.

Sending Loving-Kindness to All Living Beings

Now expand your awareness, and picture the whole world in front of you as if it were a little ball.

Send warm wishes to every living being on the planet who, like you, wants to be happy:

> *Just as I wish to, may you live with ease, happiness, and good health.*

> *Just as I wish to, may you live with ease, happiness, and good health.*

> *Just as I wish to, may you live with ease, happiness, and good health.*

Take a deep breath in. And breathe out. And another deep breath in and let it out. Notice the state of your mind and how you feel after this meditative session.

When you're ready, you may open your eyes, or if you kept them open since the beginning, you can just hold a gentle smile.

I work in a small bakery. A co-worker of mine was talking to a man online for a few months. She sent him a photo of herself and he rudely remarked at her weight. She was very hurt.
I knew she loved raspberry white chocolate scones.
I made up a batch and brought her one and said, 'This scone made me think of you. Do you know why?' She replied, 'Because they are my favourite?' And I said, 'Because this was the most beautiful scone.' Her sincere joyful response and laughter was priceless.[13]

BEFORE YOU GO

If you acquire material wealth in life, you can buy things and help those in need of financial assistance. If you build the wealth of fitness by exercising and eating right, you are rewarded with good health. Similarly, there's a way to build the wealth of kindness. It'll help you in keeping negative emotions at bay, so they don't keep bugging you. The wealth of kindness will go with you wherever you are. Here are my ten tips of acquiring and growing kindness in the course of your daily lives:

1. BE KIND TO YOURSELF

You do this by not abusing your body or feeling guilty about what you might have done in the past. Let bygones be bygones. No matter what you might have done in the past, you deserve to put that behind you and move on. Treat yourself with care. Eat well, sleep well and be well. This is how you can be kind to yourself.

2. BE KIND TO OTHERS

I read somewhere that you should always speak softly because you may have to chew your own words one day. So, speak gentle words. In *The Secret of Secrets*, Osho shares a lovely secret by Gurdjieff: postpone any negative response by 24 hours and do every positive thing immediately. When you feel hurt or down, don't pass it on, don't give it back. Just wait a little.

3. BE KIND TO THIS PLANET

We share this space with many other creatures and beings. Let's not litter and destroy this planet. We could plant more trees, restrict the use of plastic, consume less dairy (or maybe go vegan altogether) and reduce animal cruelty. Every little act matters.

4. BE KIND TO THE UNIVERSE

Just like every vehicle operating on fossil fuel, every little factory, every ounce of carbon emission adds to the global warming, every thought, every emotion we send out in the universe makes a difference. No one progresses by harbouring feelings of hatred and jealousy.

5. Be Kind on Social Media

The person reading your comments is not a robot but a real human being. There's nothing to be gained or proved by trolling someone. When we speak negatively or vent or go on a rant, it doesn't relieve us, but makes us more restless and angry. We carry those feelings into our near and distant future, and they continue to build up. No trolling. You can do better.

6. Consider Having a Pet

Pets can be real catalysts in teaching you kindness. They make your heart fill up with love and their presence has been hailed as therapeutic by numerous researchers. They teach you to share and they take your mind off negativity. You get to experience unconditional love and a constant flow of innocence from a pet. Whether you like cats or dogs, it doesn't matter. If you are not allergic to fur or pets, give it serious thought.

7. Practise Random Acts of Kindness

Don't let go off any opportunity where you can make a difference to someone's life. Whether it's just stepping back in the queue, offering your seat to an elderly person or helping someone with their luggage, each little act will make a difference to not just their life, but yours, too.

8. MEDITATE ON KINDNESS

If you could take out five minutes a day or every other day to meditate on kindness, you'll experience your hardened tendencies and negative feelings gradually melting away. Even five minutes of kindness meditation will thaw you. For the most part of our free time, knowingly or otherwise, we meditate on negative, depressing and anxious thoughts. You could gently shift your attention and meditate on kindness. It'll help you tremendously.

9. CREATE A WARM SPACE IN YOUR HEART

What do we do when we feel cold? We usually turn on the fireplace or a heater. We turn on the AC when we feel hot. We go to a spa to rejuvenate. Similarly, with the practice of kindness, you can create a warm and cozy space in your heart, a place you can go to when life feels gloomy, that sacred space you could share with a lost and lonely soul. This space is created when you practise kindness and gratitude on a daily basis.

10. DOWNLOAD THE BLACK LOTUS APP

A small group of brilliant and kind people have created this app called the Black Lotus. You can use it to do guided meditation on bliss, kindness, impermanence and many others. Not only can you see numerous suggestions of random acts of kindness you may do in your daily life, but you can also earn karma points.

Black Lotus is a community of meditators where you can see how others are meditating. You can also read their stories and acts of kindness, and share your own, too. It reminds you to set your daily goals for your spiritual growth. And the icing on the cake is the Black Lotus path that shows where you are on your spiritual journey and what milestones lie ahead. You can know more about this on www.iamblacklotus.com.

NOTES

1 Kai Kupferschmidt, 'Concentrating on Kindness', *Science*, vol. 341, no. 6152, pp. 1336–39, www.sciencemag.org. This wonderful article has been reproduced in full, in the Appendix, for your reading pleasure. Used with permission from the publisher (via RightsLink Copyright service) under a commercial book license.
2 This beautiful and touching story has been contributed by Sush Garg in the Black Lotus app.
3 This story was shared in the Black Lotus app by Karthik Sankaran. I've known Karthik for a few years and his simplicity and truthfulness never ceases to amaze me. In fact, Karthik is one of the founding members of the Black Lotus.
4 This insightful story was shared by Sadhvi Vrinda Om in the Black Lotus app. She's not just my editor on this book but of all my books published thus far. Thank you, Sadhviji! Without you, my writing wouldn't be half as good.

5 This random act of kindness was done by a Black Lotus user, Puneet Om, and logged in the app. Used with permission.

6 Florence Foster Jenkins was often mocked for her poor singing ability as she routinely sang out of tune and rhythm. In fact, she became famous for singing badly, a view she disagreed with. Even though every single person in her life discouraged her from singing, she never stopped. So much so, she even performed at Carnegie Hall, when she was seventy-six years old. Speaking about kindness, she recalls how, in 1943, she was in a taxi that crashed. After the crash she found she could sing 'a higher F than ever before'. Instead of a lawsuit against the taxicab company, she sent the driver a box of expensive cigars.

7 In *ahiṃsāsatyāsteya brahmacaryāparigrahā yamāḥ* (Yoga Sutras 2.30) and *śaucasaṃtoṣatapaḥ svādhyāyeśvarapraṇidhānāni niyamāḥ* (2.32), Patanjali mentions five kinds of moral restraints and five disciplinary vows; you can think of lifestyle or religious observances even. The five moral restraints (*yama*) are: non-violence, truthfulness, non-stealing, celibacy and non-covetousness. And the five observances (*niyama*) are cleanliness, contentment, penance, study (of the spiritual texts) and devotion to God. While one could interpret that as non-violence or non-stealing, etc., Patanjali also means kindness. In my interpretation, I'm more interested in active kindness and not merely a passive outcome. Hence, my quote on Patanjali.

8 Junabel Lorenzo shared this beautiful quote in the Black Lotus app.

9 This story of kindness was shared by Nikunj Om, a Black Lotus user.

10 Kristine Levine (kristinelevinecomedy.com), 'I'm a Little Too Fat, a Little Too Giving. I Think I Know Why',

Medium, 17 January 2019, https://medium.com/s/story/i-am-a-little-too-fat-im-a-little-too-generous-i-think-i-know-why-e97cd25b7eeb.

11 A group of Black Lotus users got together and started what they called an organized act of kindness. Three days in a week, they serve fresh khichdi to hungry and ailing children and adults outside the AIIMS hospital in Delhi. This quote was taken directly from the article titled 'Can a bunch of people make this world a better place?' Yes!' by Ruchika Garg, *Hindustan Times*, 4 January 2019, https://bit.ly/2SN1yB7.

12 Sharon Salzberg is a meditation master and a New York Times bestselling author (sharonsalzberg.com). Her guided meditation technique is being used in this book with permission.

13 This beautiful little story was shared by a Black Lotus user, Spencer Berge.

APPENDIX

Concentrating on Kindness

Tania Singer helped found the field of social neuroscience. Now she wants to apply what has been learned – by training the world to be more compassionate through meditation.

Empathy made Antoinette Tuff a minor celebrity. On 20 August, a young man armed with an AK-47 and 500 rounds of ammunition burst into the school in Decatur, Georgia, where Tuff works as a bookkeeper. It might have ended in yet another senseless mass killing if it hadn't been for Tuff 's compassionate response to the gunman, recorded in its entirety because she had dialed 911.

As the man loads his weapon, Tuff seeks a human connection with him. She talks of her own struggles, her disabled son, her divorce, her thoughts of committing suicide. Finally, she persuades him to lay down his weapon, lie down on the ground, and surrender to the police. 'I love you,' she says near the end of the call. 'You're gonna be OK, sweetheart.' (Only after the man is arrested does she break down, crying 'Woo, Jesus!') Tuff's heroic conversation, posted to the Internet, was hailed by many commentators as evidence of the power of empathy and the value of compassion. If more people were like Tuff, there would be less violence and suffering, they say.

For neuroscientist Tania Singer, that sentiment has become an ambitious research programme. Singer, a director at the Max Planck Institute for Human Cognitive and Brain Sciences in Leipzig, wants to find out if people can be trained to be more compassionate. Her programme combines rigorous neuroscience with a practice some scientists dismiss as subjective and spiritual: meditation. The effort, called the ReSource Project, involves dozens of scientists and heavy use of magnetic resonance imaging (MRI). It also includes seventeen meditation teachers and 160 participants in Leipzig and Berlin who meditate at least six days a week for nine months. Singer hopes to find a 'signature of compassion' emerging in her subjects' brains: evidence that the instinct to be kind to others can be nurtured through meditation. Singer is candid about her ultimate goal: She wants to make the world a better place.

For Singer, two interests converge in the study, which she spent five years developing. She has been a pioneer in brain studies of empathy, making her 'one of the most influential social neuroscientists in the world today,' says Richard Davidson, a psychologist who studies emotions at the University of Wisconsin–Madison. She also has a long-running interest in meditation. She tries to meditate every day, has met the Dalai Lama several times, and has been to spiritual retreats lasting months. Although compassion is the study's main focus, she also aims to discover if meditation can make people better at regulating their emotions, help them concentrate, or reduce stress.

Singer knows all of this makes some people cringe. During most of her career, she kept her interest in meditation to herself. 'When I was younger, it was unthinkable for meditation research to be taken seriously,' she says. 'I had my life as a researcher and then I had my private life, where I could follow these interests.' Even her father, Wolf Singer – a neuroscientist who until 2011 headed the Department of Neurophysiology at the Max Planck Institute for Brain Research in Frankfurt – was skeptical. 'We certainly didn't practice meditation at home,' Tania Singer says.

Ouch, that Hurt

Empathy is the bridge that allows us to cross into the territory of someone else's feelings. It establishes a connection between two people, and it's the reason we enjoy reading novels and watching movies. But empathy has long been outside the scope of neuroscience. Scientists studied what happens in the brain when someone thinks or feels, but not how we can know and feel what someone else experiences.

But in 2004, while at University College London (UCL), Singer published a landmark paper in *Science* exploring what happens in our heads when we see a loved one suffer (20 February, p. 1157). For the study, she brought couples into her lab; the woman was lying in an MRI machine, and either she or her partner, who was sitting next to the scanner, received an electric shock to the hand.

The jolts themselves activated multiple areas involved in sensing and experiencing pain, such as the sensorimotor cortex and the insula; surprisingly, observing the partner in pain engaged some of the same brain areas. Not the ones that tell you you're feeling a searing pain in your left hand, Singer says, but the 'end note' of pain, that feeling of 'ouch, that hurt.' This overlap is the root of empathy, she argues.

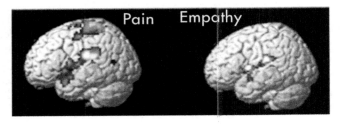

'The experiment changed how people did neuroscience,' says Chris Frith, then Singer's group leader. 'People hadn't thought before that you could study empathy in this very reductionist way,' he says. Involving more than one person at a time in an MRI study was a daring move, Frith adds. 'Tania is incredibly enthusiastic and she is prepared to deal with problems and design experiments which other people would feel are too difficult.'

Other scientists are studying the importance of empathy as well. Christian Keysers, a brain researcher at the University of Groningen in the Netherlands, is approaching the topic from a different, darker angle: he is studying imprisoned psychopaths to find out what happens when the connection between people breaks down.

In a recent paper in *Brain*, Keysers reported that there was little overlap between the brain regions active when psychopaths felt pain themselves and those lighting up when they watched videos of someone else experiencing pain. But when Keysers asked them specifically to try to empathize with the actors in the videos, the psychopaths showed the same pattern that Singer saw in her romantic couples. 'The capacity to empathize seems to be preserved in psychopaths,' Keysers says. 'They just don't use it automatically.'

Embracing Empathy

Such studies have helped to bring new attention to an age-old idea: that the world needs more love, or at least empathy. In his recent book, *The Empathic Civilization*, author Jeremy Rifkin argues that humanity needs to develop a 'global empathic consciousness' to avoid disaster. US President Barack Obama has called for a more empathic society as well; as he put it in a 2011 commencement address at Xavier University, 'When you choose to broaden your ambit of concern and empathize with the plight of others, whether they are close friends or distant strangers – it becomes harder not to act; harder not to help.' There's a more cynical way to make that case: You help someone not because you want to reduce their pain, but your own. Feel their suffering more strongly, and you are more likely to act.

For Singer, who moved from UCL to the University of Zurich in 2006 and took her current job in 2010, the interest in empathy came naturally. She has an identical twin sister, and likes to say that she was 'born as a we' and that people 'constantly resonate with each other.' What she is trying to train in the ReSource Project, however, is a slightly different capacity that she calls compassion. In daily life, the two words have overlapping meanings and they're often used interchangeably, but Singer suspects that they are two different phenomena associated with different brain activity patterns.

That insight came from her work with Matthieu Ricard, a French Buddhist monk with a background in molecular biology who lives in Nepal and practices meditation. When Singer asked Ricard to 'do his thing,' focusing on compassion, in the MRI scanner, she got a surprise. The brain regions she saw light up were not the ones that she had seen time and again when subjects tuned into the suffering of another person. Instead, areas associated with romantic love or reward, such as the nucleus accumbens and ventral striatum, were activated.

Confused, Singer asked Ricard what he had been doing. He explained that he had put himself into a state of compassion, a warm feeling of well-wishing toward the world. When Ricard went back into the scanner and concentrated on the plight of children in a Romanian orphanage he had seen in a documentary, his brain showed the typical signature of empathy. But Ricard later said that the pain quickly became unbearable. 'I felt emotionally exhausted, very similar to being burned out.'

Doctors and nurses have also reported being worn out by too much second-hand suffering. And empathy has other drawbacks, Harvard University psychologist Steven Pinker writes in an email. Corruption, for instance, is basically a result of our natural tendency to empathize more with our friends and relatives than with strangers, and to favour them at the expense of others. 'No amount of training is going to erase this difference,' Pinker writes.

Indeed, studies have shown that people are more likely to empathize with others of their own race or supporters of their favourite football team; even rats show a stronger signature of empathy toward cagemates than to other rats. The world needs justifiable policies and a robust commitment to human rights rather than more empathy, Pinker argues. 'Frankly, I don't feel empathy for every one of the two billion Indians and Chinese – who has the time or energy? But I also feel very strongly that they should not be harmed, exploited, or killed. These aren't the same thing.'

Singer, too, acknowledges the limits of empathy. After her experience with Ricard she changed tack and concentrated on compassion, Ricard's state of general warmth – which she also calls 'empathic concern,' as opposed to 'empathic distress.' 'I thought we should all be more empathic and the world would be a better place,' Singer says. 'But Ricard taught me that compassion is something completely different from empathy.' Now, she's convinced it is this 'caring system' that needs to be used more. The general warm feelings from compassion would not be limited to friends or relatives, and they are less stressful for caregivers than empathy.

Love Generation

Numerous studies have shown that people can be 'primed' to think more socially in various ways – from reading simple instructions to holding a warm cup of coffee. In one test, participants who listened to Bob Sinclar's hit song 'Love Generation' were more likely to come up with words like 'help' than those who listened to Sinclar's less uplifting song 'Rock This Party.' But Singer isn't interested in words; she wants to train people to act more socially in everyday life. And from personal experience, she believes meditation may be the way to do it.

At its most basic, the technique simply involves focusing on a feeling. In one meditation exercise in her study, participants are told to imagine a person they love and to concentrate on positive feelings toward them. 'May you be happy. May you be safe and sheltered. May you be healthy. May you live with a light heart,' the teacher intones. Like bodybuilders increasing the weights they lift, meditators can intensify their compassionate feelings over time. Expert meditators can go very far, Singer says; rape victims may meditate on feeling compassion for their rapist, for instance.

To measure meditation's effects, researchers in the ReSource Project determine the level of the stress hormone cortisol in participants' saliva, test their reaction times, have them fill out questionnaires, and shepherd them through virtual reality worlds while monitoring their heart rate. Each participant's brain is scanned for several hours five times over the course of the study.

Participants also play computer games designed to evaluate their compassion level. In one of them, developed with Swiss economist Ernst Fehr, they have to guide a smiley along a winding path that leads to a treasure chest; they have blue or red keys to open gates of the same color. But another smiley is also wandering the screen, on its own quest to another treasure, and players have to decide whether to open gates for it, too. In a preliminary study in 2011, Singer showed that just one day of compassion meditation made people more likely to help the other smiley, whereas 1 day of memory training did not.

Singer is also trying to better understand what goes on in the brain when it is feeling compassion. The activation patterns seen in the scanner leave open two possibilities: The feeling could be linked to the neurotransmitter dopamine and the brain's reward circuits (which, among many other things, makes you crave chocolate) or it could be linked to what she calls the affiliation network, which is activated for example when you view a picture of your partner or your own child, and is mediated by the neurotransmitters oxytocin or opioids.

Singer admits that pinning down the neurobiology of compassion is difficult because the mental state it corresponds to remains fuzzy. A French Buddhist monk may have a very different concept of compassion than an African doctor or a British businessman, and there's friction between the classic third person perspective of science and subjective experiences. 'But we need the first-person experience as well as the third-person science,' she says.

Wet Noodle

On an evening in early September, Singer is sitting barefoot on the floor of the Berlin apartment that she rents from Danish Icelandic artist Ólafur Elíasson, known for his mood-altering installations of water, air, and light. Beautiful globes made of wood, glass, and metal hang from the ceiling, like huge glowing molecules, as Singer talks about what compassion training, practiced on a large scale, could help achieve. At the World Economic Forum in Davos, she has spoken about 'caring economics,' based on cooperation and compassion instead of just competition. A new grant from the George Soros–backed Institute for New Economic Thinking will allow her and economist Dennis Snower of the Kiel Institute for the World Economy to outline how a compassion-based economy could work.

She has also produced a free 900 page e-book, entitled *Compassion: Bridging Practice and Science*, scheduled to go online on 18 September. Based on a 2011 Berlin workshop, it covers everything from the neuroscience of compassion and empathy to specific training schedules. Bringing together texts from Singer and others, sound collages from her twin sister, and Elíasson's photos, it shows 'that science and art are actually capable of producing things together,' Elíasson says.

Singer hopes the book will help spread her message. People think compassion makes you vulnerable for exploitation, that it is weak, that it is a 'wet noodle,' she says. 'In fact compassion is courageous, compassion is tough.' But she's aware that many of her colleagues are skeptical of her sweeping vistas – and even more about getting there through meditation.

One problem is that historically, meditation is intertwined with religion. Scientists like Singer and Davidson take care not to include religious references in their study designs; meditation practices 'offer a kind of training technology' that even strident atheists can use, Davidson says. But many meditation studies, including Davidson's, are funded by the John Templeton Foundation, a philanthropic organization that has frequently been criticized for trying to blur the boundaries between science and religion. (Davidson says that the foundation is 'doing a great service' and that the money comes with no strings attached.)

Another problem is that meditation research is not known for rigor. In 2007, scientists working for the US National Center for Complementary and Alternative Medicine sifted through more than 800 studies looking at meditation's health effects. They were not impressed. The research 'does not appear to have a common theoretical perspective and is characterized by poor methodological quality,' they wrote.

The most important problem has been that scientists fail to use adequate control groups. Many studies compare participants in a meditation program to people who applied for the study but did not take part. That leaves many factors unaccounted for, from being part of a group experience and having a devoted teacher to the fresh air at a retreat. In a 2012 paper, Davidson showed that many reported effects of 'mindfulness' meditation disappear when the control group takes part in a similar program without the specific meditation techniques. Singer hopes her own study design is rigorous enough to withstand criticism. During the first three months, both groups are trained in meditation focused on attention; then one group gets 3 months of compassion training, while the other focuses on 'perspective taking' – a way of viewing their own thoughts and feelings from a distance. If Singer sees differences between the groups after that, it will be due to the different meditation techniques, she says. 'I've had people tell me I'm crazy to use such a conservative measurement, and that I will never find anything this way,' she says. Meditation training and follow-up studies will run until 2015, but Singer expects the first results next year. Seasoned by skeptical responses, Singer has learnt not to bring up her own meditation with fellow scientists, and she is reluctant to discuss it with *Science*. But she's encouraged that many scientists have recently become more interested. Christof Koch, chief scientific officer at the Allen Institute for Brain Sciences in Seattle, Washington, for instance, says that he used to doubt the value of studying meditation. But at a meeting between Western scientists and Buddhist monks, he was impressed by the Dalai Lama and by researchers like Singer and Davidson, 'very serious basic scientists who knew their stuff.' The meeting convinced him that meditation research is worthwhile, Koch says.

Singer's father, too, changed his position, after attending a two-week meditation retreat in the Black Forest a few years ago where speaking, or even making eye contact, was forbidden. 'There is no question that meditation can lead to altered states of consciousness while you are doing it,' Wolf Singer says. He has become friends with Ricard, and a conversation between the two about meditation and brain sciences was just published as a book.

For Tania Singer, compassion research is a logical next step in neuroscience – but one that offers more hope for humanity than most other lines of research. 'Why do other people study the amygdala and research how fear works? It's basic science,' she says. 'We are researching a system that is the opposite of fear, that allows us to go in peace, to trust ourselves and others more, that breeds tolerance.'

ABOUT THE AUTHOR

Om Swami has touched the lives of millions around the world through his writings on spirituality and wellness. An MBA from University of Technology, Sydney, he has built and exited multimillion-dollar businesses. An unconventional monk, he's the brain behind the fastest-growing meditation and kindness movement in the world: Black Lotus. Om Swami writes on his blog, os.me, twice a month, and stays away from all forms of social media.

Om Swami's other bestselling books with HarperCollins include *If Truth be Told: A Monk's Memoir* (2014), *The Wellness Sense: A Practical Guide to Your Physical and Emotional Health Based on Ayurvedic and Yogic Wisdom* (2015), *When All Is Not Well: Depression, Sadness and Healing – A Yogic Perspective* (2016), *The Last Gambit* (2017), *Mind Full to Mindful: Zen Wisdom from a Monk's Bowl* (2018) and *The Children of Tomorrow: A Monk's Guide to Mindful Parenting* (2019).

Printed in Great Britain
by Amazon

46219004R00111